Dear Church:

What we want from you, church, is only one
thing—be the good news. Don't tell us about a
Christ who died two thousand years ago. Show us
a living Christ in your own personal lives. We want
no words from you except those red with the blood
of your sacrifice, not His. We don't want the word,
but the Word made flesh.
.... If you want to show us something, tear off
your mask and show us the glory of God in the
face of a sinner saved by grace. Don't give us little
things that the world can give better. We want to
know about life, love, death, heaven, and hell. If
you have some answers, share them with us.

Yours sincerely,
The World

You Can Be Born Again

by John F. Havlik

A Giniger Book
published in association with

PINNACLE BOOKS   LOS ANGELES

YOU CAN BE BORN AGAIN

A Giniger Book edition, published by special arrangement with Pinnacle Books, Inc.

ISBN: 0-523-40103-5

First Pinnacle printing, March 1978

Printed in the United States of America

PINNACLE BOOKS, INC.
One Century Plaza
2029 Century Park East
Los Angeles, California 90067

*This book is dedicated to The Honorable May-
nard Jackson, Mayor of the City of Atlanta, and
Arthur B. Rutledge, retired executive director of
the Home Mission Board.*

*To Maynard Jackson because he and I have
been neighbors, friends and fellow pilgrims. He
has assisted me in my understanding of this world
in its pain and brokenness. I have tried to assist
him in his understanding of that other world. He
has made Atlanta a better city to live in, until we
live in that city "whose Builder and Maker is
God." I hope we'll be neighbors there, too.*

*And to Arthur B. Rutledge because he has been
an example of courageous and creative leadership
in assisting me and thousands of other Southern
Baptists in applying the gospel to the anxieties of
our times. He has always been a good example of
what a "born again believer" is like.*

*All three of us are citizens of Atlanta. Daddy
King says, "Atlanta isn't heaven, but it is the next
best thing to it." These two friends share a common desire with me to make our city the city that
is too busy to hate, but not too busy to love.*

CONTENTS

PREFACE

"And the light shines in the darkness, but the darkness cannot put it out" (John 1:5). In the age of Aquarius, the sixties, when a secular theology was saying that God was dead, that light was still shining and the "now" generation was beginning to feel the breath of the Spirit.

During the Thanksgiving holidays in 1968, in Springfield, Massachusetts, where a black Cuban pastor was working with Puerto Ricans, a Georgia peanut farmer named Jimmy Carter found new meaning for his life. The rest of the Anglos stood while the Puerto Ricans knelt in prayer. But Jimmy Carter got on his knees with the Puerto Ricans. He used the Spanish he had learned in the Navy to communicate his faith. The waning years of the sixties brought religious awakening not only to Jimmy Carter but to many others.

The seventies have been called "the age of anxiety," "the age of detente" and "the age of ethnicity." But church history will probably call the period, "the age of the spirit." A new theology has emerged, a theology of experience that is emphasizing the Jesus of history, the person of the Holy Spirit, and love. Its center, from which everything else radiates, is the experience of being "born again."

Because Jimmy Carter is a Southern Baptist, new attention is being given this aggressive, growing denomination. Television and radio stations in northern cities are calling Southern Baptist pastors for interviews to explain "being born again" to listeners. However, this experience is not exclusively a Southern Baptist one. The new birth is a personal experience claimed by millions who may be Presbyterian, Methodist, Catholic, Baptist or anything else.

The roots of experiential faith centered in an experience of "new birth" and evidenced in evangelical zeal are directly related to the church of the first century and the record of that church in action in the New Testament. There is also something very American about our evangelical faith which has its roots in the period of national beginnings. If you already know about this bit of American history you may want to go on to the later chapters of this book.

Evangelical Roots

"Multitudes come, some roaring on the ground, some wringing their hands, some in ecstasies, some praying, some weeping; and others so outrageously cursing and swearing that it was thought they were really possessed of the Devil." This was the revival scene described by a visitor to a Baptist revival about 1755. The revival was conducted by an unnamed Baptist farmer-preacher in North Carolina.

The Baptists in America, if not "born in a revival," were "weaned and came of age" in a revival. The story of the persecution of Baptists in the late seventeenth century is a deplorable fact of American history. The new charter of 1691 in the Massachusetts colony, however, gave "liberty of conscience to all dissenters except Papist." In Connecticut, Baptists gained the right to worship in their own churches (1708) and were exempted from religious taxation (1729). But the lifting of persecution did not result in growth.

It was not until the "Great Awakening" (1740-43) that amazing numerical growth began. In 1740 there were only twenty-one Baptist churches in New England and eleven of the twenty-one were in Rhode Island. In the middle colonies, Baptists were strongest in Pennsylvania. The Baptists did better in the Quaker colonies, where freedom of conscience existed. By 1750, there were only three Baptist churches in Virginia because of Anglican opposition. The Carolinas were good for the Baptists and a church in Charleston may have existed as early as 1683. Though Baptists had a foothold in the southern colonies by 1750, it was not until the Separate (revivalistic) Baptists arrived that real growth began.

The Colonial Revival (the First Great Awakening) had its roots in the Old World. The German pietistic revival was brought to America by Theodore Frederick Freylinghuysen who began his ministry in 1720 in the Raritan Valley of New Jersey. Gilbert Tennant, the leading evangelist of the Presbyterians in the middle colonies, met Freylinghuysen in 1726. His famous "Log College" became a training center for the evangelistic Presbyterians. The third influence for revival was the Wesleyan Awakening in England. The person who tied the Colonial Revival together was George Whitefield, a Methodist. From 1738 to 1770, he made seven journeys to America with preaching itineraries ranging from Maine to Georgia. It was said that Whitefield did not have "a theological bone in his body or hair on his head." He was comfortable with the Calvinist Jonathan Edwards, Gilbert Tennant and Jenkins Jones, pastor of a Baptist church in Philadelphia. Methodists, Presbyterians, Dutch Reformed and Baptists were among the instruments of revival.

Shubal Stearns, a Baptist minister from Connecticut, came to Virginia where he was joined by his brother-in-law, Daniel Marshall. These men were Separate Baptists after being converted in the revival in New England. Hindered by opposition in Virginia, they went to Sandy Creek, in Guilford County, North Carolina. The coming of these two revivalistic Baptists marks the beginning of revival for Baptists in the South. Their church grew from sixteen members, including the families of Stearns and Marshall, to six hundred members in a short time. Morgan Edwards, in *History of the Baptists in North Carolina,* says the Sandy Creek church: "is the mother of all the Separate Baptists. From this Zion went forth the Word, and great was the company of those who published it. This church in seventeen years had spread her branches southward as far as Georgia, eastward to the sea and Chesapeake Bay, and northward to the waters of the Potomac. In seventeen years she became grandmother to forty-two churches from which sprang one hundred twenty-five ministers, many of whom are ordained."

The Baptist revivalists were not without opposition. They were opposed by the Regular Baptists, the Anglicans and the middle class. They were considered ignorant, uncouth and crude. Most of them had little or no formal education. W. W. Sweet, in *Religion in Colonial America,* records that Elder David Barrow, a Virginia Baptist preacher, was invited by a friend to preach outdoors at the mouth of the James River. He was met at the river by a large gang of "well-dressed men" who took Barrow and, in mockery of immersion, repeatedly doused him in the water and mud until he was nearly drowned. The same arguments used in New England against the revivalists a generation before were used against the Baptists in the South. But revival went on with decreasing power until the light of it was almost extinguished by the American Revolution.

After the Revolution, evangelical zeal and experiential faith in Jesus Christ became focused in the great camp meetings. The day for an American revival camp meeting began at daybreak with the sounding of a trumpet, a call to family prayer. The camp meetings occupied three to five acres along the bank of a stream where there was water for the people and horses. It is difficult to set an exact date for these camp meeting revivals, but they had a standard form by 1799, and reached the peak of their popularity by 1825. D. A. Johnson, in his *Frontier Camp Meeting*, says, "The Great Awakening (Second) which began after the Revolution was primarily centered in the camp meeting. It was an American phenomenon in the revivalism that was destined to really change the face of religion in America."

According to one writer: "The frontier was crude, turbulent, and godless. Evangelical protestantism more than any other single force tamed it." Unbelief was a way of life. Thomas Paine's *Age of Reason* was at the zenith of its popularity. Hard liquor was plentiful and cheap, and even the professing Christians drank heavily. Drink was a curse on the frontier. Every social affair, including barn raisings, log rollings, baptisms and wakes were occasions for hard drinking. Stores gave customers a free drink with every fifty-cent purchase. Easterners were shocked at the drunkenness and brutality of the frontier. One witness says, "Tearing, kicking, scratching, biting and gouging each other's eyes by dexterous use of the thumb and finger were common on the frontier."

Although the Methodists most widely used the camp meeting, John Waller, a Separate Baptist minister, conducted some of the first camp meetings. He was probably the first to call his outdoor revivals "camp meetings." Samuel Harriss, James Reed and many other Baptist preachers who used the camp meeting were influenced by the prerevolutionary revival in Guilford County, North Carolina. These Baptist revivals were in many ways the prototype of the great camp meetings that took place after the Revolution.

Every camp meeting had ground rules that were strictly followed. The Baptist camp meeting rules in Waller's revivals were as follows:

1. No female on any account shall be permitted to appear in the camp until an hour after sunrise in the morning nor stay later than an hour before sunset at night.
2. The persons in the camp shall depend for sustenance during the camp meeting on the friendly hospitality of the neighborhood.
3. Any person in the camp awakening at any period during the night may pray or sing without disturbing the slumber of others.

The general camp meeting was the greatest of all. Baptists, Methodists and Presbyterians worked side by side, and the crowds were measured in the thousands. James McCready, one great camp meeting preacher, said, "Bigotry and prejudice have received a death wound. . . ." Presbyterians and Methodists loved one another. In these meetings there were three services a day at eight o'clock, eleven o'clock and one o'clock in the afternoon. The "biggest gospel gun" was saved for the eleven o'clock service. The powerful sermons from some of these great services still survive. A witness described one of the services as follows:

After the meeting the power of the Almighty came down in such a wonderful manner as is seldom witnessed. Brother Harriss fell back from the pulpit, overcome by the influence of the Holy Spirit, and called upon me to invite the people forward for prayers. . . . The invitation was no sooner extended than the mourners came pouring forward in a body for prayer until the altar was filled with weeping penitents.

The camp meeting preachers all emphasized the same themes—universal redemption, free and full salvation, justification by faith, regeneration by the Holy Ghost and the joy of a living religion. The preachers were often rough and crude, but so were the times in which they lived and preached. These great camp meetings, which lasted as late as 1840, helped tame the American frontier and made it a fit place to live and rear children.

A Lay Theology of Experience

The preachers of the First and Second Great Awakenings were for the most part lay preachers with no theological training. Their emphasis on "new birth" and their evangelical zeal spread among Baptists from Sandy Creek, North Carolina, southwestward along the Piedmont into Georgia, Alabama and Mississippi and westward into the Kentucky and Tennessee frontier. As we have already said, revivalism had its roots in the Wesleyan revival that shook two continents. That revival was really born when Peter Bohler, a Moravian, asked John Wesley, a member and priest of the Church of England, "Have you been born again?" At Aldersgate, on May 24, 1738, Wesley experienced a new birth and the greatest revival in the history of the church was on the agenda of history.

This new Christian theology of experience is a lay theology. It is unwritten and draws persons together around a common spiritual experience rather than a creed or a dogma.

Although Southern Baptists did not discover the "new birth" they are a good example of persons drawn together by a common experience. Others often wonder how Southern Baptists can have such unity and loyalty amid great diversity. Southern Baptist churches are both elitist and egalitarian, segregated and multiracial (of thirty thousand churches, twenty-eight hundred are ethnic and five hundred black), rich and poor, and among their members are numbered both the educated and the uneducated. The unifying force is a common experience with Jesus Christ in which He is "both Lord and Savior."

It must also be said that this is true of other groups of Christians as well as Southern Baptists.

The lay theology of experience focusing on the new birth is particularly relevant in several ways. First, if the church is to evangelize, the present generation must be able to speak its faith in clear, simple language. Communication is helping other people understand the meanings words have for us. The problem with most Christian theology is that it is so blurred by a technical vocabulary and philosophical distinctions that it is hardly comprehensible to the listener or reader. Indeed, in reading Christian theology one wonders if the author himself understands what he is talking about. This is especially true of the "sermon" as delivered in the average congregation.

In contrast, the lay theology of experience speaks of a personal relationship with Jesus Christ in terms that we use every day for other interpersonal relationships. A case in point is "being born again." The words we ordinarily use to describe our introduction into our family are used to describe our introduction into the family of God. Becoming a Christian is "knowing" Jesus Christ, "loving" Him and "following" Him. The experience of coming to know Him, to love Him, and to follow Him is so life-changing, so dramatic, so revolutionary, that it is like being born all over again.

If, in relationship to the world, the church must be able to state its faith in clear, simple language, in relationship to itself, it must not continue to be "picky" about little things. The church spends a lot of time and energy defending the color of its robes, the correctness of its liturgy and the fine points of its theology. The church is too often represented by evangelists and missionaries who spend more energy telling the world why some rival sect or denomination is wrong rather than talking about a new birth of love, meaning and joy in Jesus Christ.

Thousands of Christian lay people are discovering a new commonality in the experience of the new birth. Little differences are laid aside for a celebration of common life in Jesus Christ. Many retreat centers today are crowded with Christians from many denominations united in love and devotion to Christ. The world is beginning to see a church united in a common experience shared by persons from many denominations, and to hear that loving Jesus Christ means loving all His followers everywhere with no reference to denominational affiliation. There is hope in this that the church will present a united, loving front to the world of unbelievers.

With respect to the fellowship of believers there must be practice as well as preaching. The Word must become flesh. The new lay theology of experience speaks to this need in the church. Those who are born again emphasize Christlike living rather than doctrinal correctness as living proof of the power of the gospel of Jesus Christ. The person who is not a Christian is not interested in what we believe but rather in how we live. How do we deal with sin and temptation? Does our faith give our lives meaning and purpose? Has our faith given new dimension to our family life? What does our faith do for us in our work? These are the questions that the person out of Christ wants to have answered. In this regard, the lay-oriented theology that focuses on being born again is truly relevant. Because it is experiential, it is related to all the experiences of life.

Recently, in Minneapolis, I heard an eighteen-year-old girl give her testimony. She obviously had no knowledge of the "language of Zion" so prevalent in the Southern "Bible Belt." She said, "Three months ago I didn't care nothin' about nothin'. Then I was born again. Now I care about me, my family and my friends." She related her experience not to a creed or a denomination but to her interpersonal relationships. That's where it's at!

Finally, in relation to the individual believer, evangelism requires personal commitment. And it is commitment to a person, Jesus Christ. The church cannot "sell" Southern culture and Jesus Christ, or WASP culture and Jesus Christ, or capitalism and Jesus Christ. Our message is Christ and nothing else, Christ and nothing less, Christ and nothing more. What we have to sell is our "Love Story." God loved the world so much He gave His Son. Christ loved the world so much He died. God loves me so much He has come to me through His Spirit. When I am personally related to Christ through a new birth it is not just a religious experience, it is a love relationship with God and Christ. It is my commitment to Him that is important. I know He wants me to share His love. It is news that is too good to keep quiet. When lay people who are sincere in loving begin sharing their faith in the normal pattern of their lives, revival and renewal come as natural consequences.

My Personal Testimony

I would be very remiss in my obligation as a Christian writer if I sent this book on its mission without sharing with my readers my own personal experience of new birth.

I am a first-generation American. I was born in Milwaukee, Wisconsin, where my family lived without any real connection with a Christian church. When I was a teen-ager, we moved to Tulsa, Oklahoma. It was there that one of my sisters and I were deeply influenced by a group of Christians from a nearby church. In a gospel meeting under a tent, I experienced a new birth and Christ came into my life. I did not become perfect nor am I perfect now, but my life has never been the same since that time. For me, it was a new birth of love, joy, peace and hope. Christ gave meaning and purpose to my existence. From that time I have known who I am, why I am here and where I am going. I entered into a trust relationship with Jesus Christ.

Since that time, forty-one years ago, many things have happened to me. I have four earned degrees, including three graduate degrees. I have traveled over a great deal of the world. I have never seen anything or heard anything that would make me believe that what happened to me when I gave my life to Christ was anything less than a new birth. To God be the glory!

And now, dear reader, I have a prayer for you. It is the prayer of Paul that he prayed for the Christians at Ephesus:

"For this reason, I bow my knees before the Father, from whom every family in heaven and on earth derives its name, that He would grant you, according to the riches of His glory, to be strengthened with power through His Spirit in the inner man; so that Christ may dwell in your hearts through faith; and that you, being rooted and grounded in love, may be able to comprehend with all the saints what is the breadth and length and height and depth, and to know the love of Christ which surpasses knowledge, that you may be filled up to all the fullness of God." (Ephesians 3:14-19 NASB)

Brother John

Atlanta, Georgia
March, 1978

ACKNOWLEDGMENTS

I would be guilty of ingratitude if I did not express my appreciation to Miss Janice Trusty, who typed my manuscript and discovered many of my blunders; to my wife, Anna Mae, who read the manuscript; and to my publishers, The K. S. Giniger Company and Pinnacle Books, who agreed with changes that I made in our original "game plan" for this book. I am also grateful for the understanding and patience of my supervisor at the Home Mission Board, C. B. Hogue, in putting up with my preoccupation and lapses of memory for a period of seven weeks.

A Note for Theologians

I am sure that I will be chided for ascribing human characteristics to God. I am deeply indebted to Paul Tillich for some concepts in my chapter, "A New Birth of Love," but I do not share Tillich's fears of understanding God in the way we view human relationships. I am indebted to many others for insights, ideas, thoughts and concepts, and have tried to follow the example of Jesus in communicating my understanding of God in terms of human life and experience.

I did not attempt to write this book as scholastic theology. It is intended for communicating spiritual truth to the person without knowledge of theology.

I have depended upon my own knowledge of the Greek text for some free translations of passages of the New Testament, and accept responsibility for them. All Scripture translations are my own unless indicated by the standard references, NASB for *The New American Standard Bible,* TEV for *Today's English Version (Good News Bible),* and AV for the Authorized Version (King James Bible).

If only one person made in God's image finds himself and finds God in an experience of "new birth" as a result of this book it will be successful in its mission.

J. F. H.

YOU CAN BE BORN AGAIN

I never thought Joe would leave me. After twenty-eight years, how could he do this to me? I'm ashamed to see Gordon and Frances in Chicago. How can I ever tell them? Stewardess, please give me another martini. I really loved that man and I think I told him so almost every day. He never said that to me very often, less and less as time went on. I guess he just got tired of me. O God, I knew about it. I knew about her. I have known for a long time. I just couldn't face him and talk about it. Maybe I should have talked to him about it when I first knew it was happening. You just don't talk about a thing like that.

God, I wish this plane would crash. I wonder if he would care? Maybe he will come back to me someday? I'd like to be able to tell him that I wouldn't take him back, that I no longer care. I would take him back. I just can't help it. I love him. I will always love him. God, how that hurts, to love someone who doesn't love you. A lot of it was my fault. I was always complaining. We just seemed to lose touch. I hate you, Joe, I hate you.

I can't forget what Frances said—did Joe and I leave God out of our lives? What does God care about me? Would that have made any difference? In her last letter, Frances said she was praying for me. God, if you're out there in those clouds I see below, I sure could use some help. Frances said in her letter that I could be "born again" and that life could begin again. I wonder if it can.

1.

LIFE CAN BEGIN AGAIN

"Now it came about that while the multitude were pressing around Him and listening to the word of God, He was standing by the lake of Gennesaret; and He saw two boats lying at the edge of the lake; but the fishermen had gotten out of them, and were washing their nets.

"And He got into one of the boats, which was Simon's, and asked him to put out a little way from the land. And He sat down and began teaching the multitudes from the boat. And when He had finished speaking, He said to Simon, 'Put out into the deep water and let down your nets for a catch.'

"And Simon answered and said, 'Master, we worked hard all night and caught nothing, but at Your bidding I will let down the nets.' And when they had done this, they enclosed a great quantity of fish; and their nets began to break; and they signaled to their partners in the other boat, for them to come and help them. And they came, and filled both of the boats, so that they began to sink.

"But when Simon Peter saw that, he fell down at Jesus' feet, saying, 'Depart from me, for I am a sinful man, O Lord!' For amazement had seized him and all his companions because of the catch of fish which they had taken; and so also James and John, sons of Zebedee, who were partners with Simon.

"And Jesus said to Simon, 'Do not fear, from now on you will be catching men.' And when they had brought their boats to land, they left everything and followed Him" (Luke 5:1-11 NASB).

Recently, a lovely young woman asked to see me after a gospel service. She told me that her marriage had just ended in a divorce court. She said, "I feel I have failed. My life is ruined." She related how hard she had struggled to make her marriage a success. Something good and beautiful had turned into a hell on earth. She said, "I know I haven't been perfect, but God knows I have tried. He just came home one evening and told me he just didn't care anymore. I did everything I knew how to do. Nothing worked. I have failed. That's it, I am a failure."

This was exactly how the four fishermen felt. They had worked hard all night. They were bone weary when they beached their boats that morning. They were failures. Because they were fishermen and knew the ways of the sea, they would go out again. But they had known many nights like this. Sometimes it seemed that they could barely keep food on the table and a roof over their heads. Jesus often came down to the beach to see the boats leave in the evening and return in the morning. He saw and knew the agony of the four fishermen. Before they had time to tie down the boats He took a seat and said, "Go out in the deep water and put down your nets."

Mary, the lovely young woman whose marriage fell apart, and Simon Peter had the same problem. When I said to her, "Life can begin again, dear," she said, "I don't see how. I have tried everything."

Simon Peter said, "We have worked hard all night

2

and now you tell us to go out again? We know when the fish are not running. What do you know about fishing?" But then, because Peter knew Jesus, he grudgingly said, "Okay, we'll do it because You say so."

I told Mary that Christ wanted to come into her life and give her love, joy and peace. I told her how Christ can make life begin again. I took Mary to the gospel of John, chapter four, and introduced her to the woman of Samaria, saying, "Mary, here is a woman who tried several marriages and none of them worked. She finally got so desperate and lonely she tried sex without marriage. She was so ashamed that she would not go to the well for water early in the morning and late in the evening for fear of meeting the other women." We read together the conversation of Jesus with the woman. We shared the excitement and joy of the woman over her new found faith. I said, "Mary, do you see that Jesus, who is our Lord and Savior, wants to come into your life so that life can begin again as it did for the woman at the well?"

She said, "Yes, but how can this happen to me?" I then took Mary to the Gospel of Luke, chapter five, and introduced her to Simon Peter. I reminded Mary that the woman at the well and Simon Peter both found a new life so new and exciting and different that the only way to describe it is to say that it is like being born all over again.

"Mary," I asked, "have you been born again?"

She answered, "I am a member of a church, but I know that I haven't lived right some of the time."

I told Mary that what I was really talking about was accepting Jesus Christ as her own personal Savior and beginning to follow Christ as His disciple. I showed her how Simon Peter had said, "I'll do it because You say so."

"Mary, you know that you are a sinner, as we all

3

are," I continued. "Now will you let Him into your life so that life can begin again?"

Mary said she was ready to accept Christ in her life and we prayed a prayer of commitment together. She looked up from her prayer posture when we finished praying and she said, "It's gone."

I asked, "What's gone, Mary?"

She replied, "The guilt is gone, the load is gone. I feel so new."

I then helped Mary to see that, like Simon Peter, as a new child of God she was beginning to follow Christ as His disciple. I reminded her that there was a lot to learn and experience in Christ.

Peter testifies much later in his life to the experience of being born again. "Since you have in obedience to the truth purified your souls for a sincere love of the brethren, fervently love one another from the heart, for you have been born again not of seed which is perishable but imperishable, that is through the living and abiding word of God" (I Peter 1:22,23).

Mary, after three years of new life in Christ, is enthusiastic about her experience. The child of God by the new birth, like the child by physical birth, has a lot of growing to do.

Peter at Pentecost (Acts 3) has a lot more stature as a follower of Christ than he had in the courtyard of the high priest (Matthew 26:69-74). His late epistles show much more depth than his appearances in the gospels. Peter talks about this growing process in his first epistle: "Therefore, putting aside all malice and all guile and hypocrisy and envy and all slander, like newborn babes, long for the pure milk of the word, that by it you may grow in respect to salvation" (I Peter 2:1,2 NASB).

For Mary, too, her new birth experience was the beginning of a growth process. She is learning how to share her faith and is quite busy working with young people as a warm and loving counselor. Mary and Peter are still Mary and Peter. The new birth does not mean that we lose our personality or that we become automatons or puppets with God pulling the strings. According to tradition, Peter died with the same impetuosity that was in evidence before his experience of new birth. Mary is still working on her "short fuse," which she admits was part of her problem. Mary, Peter and all of us who have experienced new birth could use the sign attached to us that says, "Be patient with me; God is not through with me yet." A variation of that sign might read, "If you think I'm terrible now, you should have met me before God started working on me."

A Piece of the Rock

At Caesarea Philippi (Matthew 16) Jesus gave Simon his new name, Peter, "the rock." He was the one who first said of Jesus, "You are the Christ, the Son of the living God." He was like a rock as the preacher at Pentecost (Acts 2) and he was like a rock in his traditional death when he requested to be crucified head downward because he was unworthy to die as the Lord had, erect. What happened on the beach of the lake of Tiberius (also called Galilee and Gennesaret) was the beginning of his becoming rock-like. From that time until this, millions have found their "piece of the Rock" in a new birth. All over this world are persons who have found "the pearl of great price" and "the treasure hid in the field." They have discovered the way of gladness and joy. As paupers, they have given Christ their lives and, as princes, they have received a new name. Their names have been changed because their lives have been changed. They

5

now take the name of "Christian" or "believer" or "follower of the Way" with meaning and power.

The modern disciples like Mary, whose real name I could not use, are not very different from Peter and the other disciples who followed our Lord during His earthly ministry. Competitive John, compulsive Peter and critical Thomas were all among His disciples. He never poured them into a mold or "brainwashed" them. They did not have a "party line" that they repeated like robots when called upon. They argued among themselves just as real people do. They were not sure about everything, but they were sure about Him. They knew that they would never be the same after they were born again. He loved them all just as they were. They were in the process of being made new. All of them had discovered that the initial shock of knowing Him was like being born all over again. They all discovered that life can begin again. I asked some of these modern disciples, "What is the new birth? What is it like to be born again?" All of them had a "piece of the Rock" and with their permission I am using their real names.

William "Bill" Bangham is an academic assistant in The Department of Biological Sciences at Georgetown University, Washington, D.C. He says, "The meaning of new birth for me is more related to life style than anything else. Just off the top of my head—thinking of my own experience—it has meant an evolving, developing life style from initial excitement and emotion to a growing experience. It is being aware of what seems to be coming up each day and beyond into the years ahead. It is finding out that I am a special, gifted person of God. It is knowing that there is meaning in life itself. It is excitement and challenge —things for me to do and situations for me to plug into. It means that God is alive and real. I am beginning to see the face of God as I walk through my own life."

Susie Harris is director of educational services at the Hall County Hospital in Gainesville, Georgia. She talks freely about her new birth experience, saying, "It means to me that first I have died to myself and with that death all my sin and guilt was buried—past, present and future. I have been made free to be open and honest with God. I no longer have to worry about what other people think. It means that I have a new awareness of who I am, a child of God watched over by His angels, an heir of God and a joint heir with Christ. Experiencing His love made me able to love others with no strings attached. The Spirit of Jesus has come into me to direct my whole life. Each day becomes an adventure when you know that Jesus has arranged all the circumstances and goes through the day with you. Being born again does not mean that I have no fun in life, for I now have the capacity to enjoy all of life and even the simplest of life's experiences takes on an exciting quality. It means a challenge to total commitment. It is a challenge to put my life on the line reaching other persons with the Good News."

Chuck Brodish is a corporate investment officer for the First National Bank of Seattle, Washington. He says that new life in Christ "is just like my physical birth. It is birth into a spiritual world of spiritual realities. I have to grow into knowledge of this spiritual world just as I had to grow into knowledge of the physical world. I see it also as a change of ownership and a change of obedience. Once I directed my own life and was obedient to my own desires. Now I realize Christ is the owner of all that I am and have and I am obedient to Him rather than letting self rule my life."

W. A. Howell and his wife Nancy are born again Christians. He is a mechanic for Delta Airlines. They preferred to speak as one because they feel that their experience in Christ is something they have always shared with one another. They say, "To us being a born again Christian is the discovery that we are the unique children of God. It is something that has happened over a period of time. Our experience is a growing and developing experience." Nancy describes her experience as "an awareness of life that I have not known before—life is more joyous, the sky bluer, the grass greener, people lovelier. And I feel a love and peace within that can only come from Jesus." The Howells both make it clear that you never really arrive—you are always in the making as a Christian. They see it as a new birth into a world of spiritual realities; a constant growth in appreciation of these realities. They conclude their witness by saying, "Our Creator waits for us to be born again as earthly fathers wait for the birth of their children."

W. E. Lewis, a builder in Nashville, Georgia, says that being born into the family of God means everything to him. He says, "It means a personal knowledge of Jesus Christ as Lord and Savior. I am no longer the same man I was before I came into this relationship with Christ. There is a wonderful relationship between Christ and myself. It is a relationship that gets better with each passing day. It is a relationship that helps me every day, not just one day. I mean that what I have is not just something you need on the day of judgment. It is something good every day. I am now a part of the family of God and I am an heir of all the spiritual riches He has stored up for me."

In a great art museum, one painting was recognized to be the work of a master but was considered one of his inferior works. While cleaning it, the museum discovered that another artist had touched up the master's work. When that paint was removed, there was the work of the master, not one of his inferior works, but one of his very best.

Back to the original. Strip off the hypocrisies. See the true humanity created in the image of God. Not the stupid anthropoid blowing his mind on drugs or alcohol. Not the bestial sex deviate drowning himself in pornography. See the real man. The man made for God. The man transformed by the grace of God.

Man has debauched, degraded, and even denied the image of God in himself. That man can change is the overwhelming gracious Good News of the believer. The transformation that Christ works in human life is the thing that authenticates that Good News. One of the keys to the Kingdom is certainly the transformed lives of believers fleshed out before the world. This makes the gospel believable. Without this authentication the gospel is only empty words.

The changing power of Jesus Christ is contagious. It spreads from heart to heart and life to life. This transforming power is one of the keys to the Kingdom of God. The church that produces such changed lives, through the proclamation of the Word, the witness of its members and its loving Christlike ministry, has this key. Bill says that conversion is "being aware that I am a special, gifted person of God." For him conversion is a discovery of self. Susie says that it is "experiencing love that has made me able to love others without any strings attached." For her the new birth is experiencing love. Chuck says, "The new birth is a change of ownership." For him it is finding a new Master. Nancy says it is "an awareness of life . . . people are lovelier . . . grass is greener . . . the sky is bluer." For her it is loving life. W. E. says, "I am not the same old man." For him it is changing direction. None of these modern disciples claims to be perfect or to have all the answers. None of them expresses the change in terms of organized religion. Yet all of them are faithful members of a congregation of believers. They are believable, "for real" people.

Birth into a Family

All of Christ's disciples, both ancient and modern, speak of their new birth as a birth into a family, the family of God. Peter, in his epistles, talks about "beloved brother, Paul." The New Testament is full of references to "Father," "brother," "children," and "my little children." None of the believers that I quoted earlier were "loners."

A great illustration of this is found in the new birth experience of Saul of Tarsus. On the Damascus road, the archenemy of the Christians thinks to win against Jesus Christ, but, instead, is won over by Him. Saul finds refuge in the house of Judas the tanner on a street called Straight in the city of Damascus. Ananias, a devout Christian, is sent to Saul by the Holy Spirit. He finds Saul of Tarsus blind in the house of Judas and, laying hands on him, he says, "Brother Saul, receive your sight" (Acts 9:17). By faith, Ananias accepts the chief persecutor of the church as a brother. Peter, in his first epistle, writes to the family of God "who reside as aliens scattered throughout Pontus, Galatia, Cappadocia, Asia, and Bithynia" (I Peter 1:1 NASB). He writes to them about the experience that has bound them together as the family of God. "Blessed be the God and Father of our Lord Jesus Christ, who according to His great mercy has caused us to be born again to a living hope through the resurrection of Jesus Christ from the dead" (I Peter 1:3 NASB).

All well-ordered families operate under two disciplines, authority and love. The authority for the family of God is Jesus Christ. "And He put all things in subjection under His feet, and gave Him as head over all things to the church, which is His body, the fulness of Him who fills all in all" (Ephesians 1:22,23 NASB). "I, therefore, the prisoner of the Lord, entreat you to walk in a manner worthy of the calling with which you have been called, with all humility and gentleness, with patience, showing forbearance to one another in love" (Ephesians 4:1,2 NASB).

Every local congregation of believers ought to be a nurturing family for the new babes in Christ. The family provides food and shelter. The family teaches good health habits. The family provides education. The family supports the weaker members. A good family gets ready for the birth of a baby.

Many churches are ill-prepared to nourish and sustain new life in Christ. All the persons we interviewed about the new birth spoke highly of their own church in terms of its supportive role. Is the church teaching the Word of God, the food for believers? Is the church assisting new believers to discover good spiritual health through proper spiritual diet and exercise? Is the church forgiving and supportive when the new believer makes mistakes? These are pointed questions the church must face if it is to be a "nursery for the newly born."

How Can I Find Christ?

You may be saying, "Well all of this is very good, but how can I find Christ so I can be born again?" You will not find Him. He will find you.

Isn't this exactly what happened to Simon Peter? What was it that made Jesus find him on the beach that morning? What was there about him that attracted Christ to him?

Sometimes people go from church to church trying to find Christ, and are disappointed. He finds us when

11

we feel our need for Him. Sometimes He finds us when we feel our need for "something" beyond us and above us and we hardly know what it is.

There is a beautiful incident in the life of Christ in Mark 5:24-34. A woman intruded into a crowd around Jesus, reached out and touched His garment in hope that this would cure her bleeding tumor. In the eyes of her society this was terrible, because she was unclean and her touch would contaminate. Instead of receiving a rebuke, however, she was healed. She never spoke His name. She just heard reports of what He could do for her, and her little bit of faith was rewarded. She was one of society's "losers." She had one new ray of hope that life could begin again when the Galilean healer came to town.

He finds us wherever we are when that need comes for us to reach out to the Word from Beyond, incarnate love, Jesus the Christ. To the woman of Samaria (John 4) who asked that very question, "Where can I find Him?" Jesus said, "We do not worship God in this mountain or in Jerusalem, but those who worship the Father worship Him in spirit and in truth."

Jesus was saying God comes to us when we need Him and when we know Him as the way and truth and life. No matter where it is, it is at that point that life can begin again.

He always comes to us at the point of our greatest need. With the woman at the well of Sychar, it was her shame because of her immoral life. With the rich young ruler, it was his inordinate love of money. With Nicodemus, it was his pride. He met each of these at the point of their need. Two of them found new life in Christ and one of them went away without Him because he loved gold more than he loved God.

Jesus Christ comes to us when there is any trace of our need for Him. He makes no conditions except our need for Him and then He is there in love ready to give us His peace.

12

So many see Christianity in abstract terms as the hope of civilization or as a religious anchor for all that is good in American civilization. These persons miss Him by a thousand miles. He only wants to come into our lives in a new birth of love, joy and peace. He wants to take us to heaven. He wants to teach us in His church the tremendous value of a human soul. And in doing this he will give society and the world the kind of person who will make any community, city, or state a better and safer place to live. He says to us, "I'll find you when life without me is unbearable —when you cannot live without me."

When Peter felt a sense of failure and a longing for something better and surer, Jesus came to him. There never has been a greater "loser" than the importunate woman in Luke 18. She had lost her husband and her son, and now she was about to lose her property to an unscrupulous person. Her only hope was an unjust judge, but, because he was her only hope, she went to him anyway. Jesus, in telling this parable, was saying to us that God may seem like an unjust judge to us in our sin, but in desperation we go to Him anyway. It is then that we discover that God is a loving Father and not at all as we thought Him to be. When my friend Mary's marriage made her think she was a "loser" and she reached out just a little for Jesus Christ, He came to her. One may say, "But I am not a loser. Look at the money I have. See my house; it is very expensive. Everything I do turns to money." You know, even with all that, you are a loser if you lose your soul.

Jesus said, "What will it profit you, if in the end you lose your soul?" You may have everything that the world calls success. Then someday you may realize that, even with all you have, you are not right with God. If then you reach out to Christ with even a trace of faith, He will come to you and offer you eternal life through a new birth. And the choice will be yours.

13

What Must I Do?

The new birth is the work of the Holy Spirit when one receives Christ as Lord and Savior. Accepting Jesus Christ as Lord and Savior, as an act of our will, produces the Holy Spirit's work of new birth. "But as many as received Him, to them He gave the right to become children of God, even to those who believe in His name, who were born not of blood, nor of the will of the flesh, nor of the will of man, but of God" (John 1:12, 13). You are not a child of God because your parents were Christians ("not of blood") and you are not a Christian because some ecclesiastical official says you are ("not of the will of man"), but because you are born of God.

This is the reason Jesus said to Nicodemus, "You must be born again" (John 3:7). Nicodemus thought that having the blood of Abraham in his veins would make him acceptable to God. But acceptance is not because of blood. John Wesley thought being properly baptized in the Anglican faith and being ordained its priest was enough. Peter Bohler asked him, "Have you been born again?" The will of man is not enough.

Peter again gives us the answer. When Jesus says, "Put out in the deep water and let down the nets," Peter argues with himself and with the Savior. He adds, however, "Okay, if you say so I'll do it." The Bible says, "Nevertheless at thy word." This is the one thing we must do—accept Him at His word. When we do this we put ourselves on the line. We say, "I do not understand it all, but I will try God. I will accept Him at His word and commit myself to Him."

The Bible says that I am a sinner. "For all have sinned and fall short of the glory of God" (Romans

14

3:23 NASB). The Bible says that the result of sin is separation from God (spiritual death). "For the wages of sin is death, but the free gift of God is eternal life in Christ Jesus our Lord" (Romans 6:23 NASB). The Bible says that Jesus Christ offers me eternal life in a new birth if I will commit my life to Him (believe). "And as Moses lifted up the serpent in the wilderness, even so must the Son of Man be lifted up; that whoever believes may in Him have eternal life. For God so loved the world that He gave His only begotten Son, that whoever believes in Him should not perish, but have eternal life" (John 3:14-16 NASB). We must accept His word at face value and dare to step out on His word by faith. God has given us His Son who offers us eternal life. If we do not believe that, then we have made God a liar because we do not believe that God will give us eternal life through a new birth if we trust Him. "The one who believes in the Son of God has the witness in himself; the one who does not believe God has made Him a liar, because he has not believed in the witness that God has borne concerning His Son. And the witness is this, that God has given us eternal life, and this life is in His Son" (I John 5:10,11 NASB).

How Can I Know?

One of the controlling factors in any birth is the law of heredity. We become like the being from which our life has come. Because the new life that we have is the life of God given to us through Christ at the new birth it is clear that our life ought to be Christlike. "For whom He foreknew, He also predestined to become conformed to the image of His Son, that He might be

15

the first-born among many brethren" (Romans 8:29 NASB). Notice that it is "to become conformed." It is a process of growth into His image. The new birth is only the beginning of life.

This is the reason that a study of His word is so important. How can we know if we are like Him if we do not know what He is like? What did Jesus do and say? This is a critical study for the new believer and it is critical for Christian preaching. One of the reasons many new believers fail to grow is that they hear sermons about the Bible and about Jesus, but not very much as to how He acted and what He said in plain simple language. One of the reasons that all new Christians should have one of the good modern versions of the New Testament is that they might understand exactly what Jesus did and what He said. What did Jesus say about poor people? How did He act toward them? What was His attitude toward sick people? Did the mentally deranged repel or attract Him? How did He treat His enemies? Did He despise the Samaritans as did most of the Jews during His day? How did He treat a woman discovered in the very act of adultery? How did He feel about money? Did He like children? All of these questions can be answered from reading about Jesus in the New Testament. Then we can decide if His life is in us.

The First Epistle of John was written "that you may know," while his gospel was written "that you may believe." "Whoever believes that Jesus is the Christ is born of God; and whoever loves the Father loves the child born of Him. By this we know that we love the children of God, when we love God and observe His commandments. . . . For whatever is born of God overcomes the world; and this is the victory that has overcome the world——our faith. . . . These things I have written to you who believe in the name of the Son of God, in order that you may know that you have

16

eternal life" (I John 5:1-13 NASB). The born again person believes that Jesus is the Christ. We believe that He is the One promised by the prophets, the Son of God and Savior of sinners.

If we have been born again, we will love the children of God. This means all of His children. We will not want to know the color of their skin or the slant of their eyes, or the position they occupy socially or economically. Are they God's children? We will love them because He loves them and they are our spiritual "kinfolk."

We can know we are born again because we keep His commandments. On one occasion, He said there are only two that sum up all the rest. To love God with all our being and to love our neighbor as ourselves. In the parable of the good Samaritan (Luke 10) He told us that our neighbor was anyone we meet who is in need.

We know we have been born again because we overcome the world. We will not win every battle but we will win the war. All of these are tests by which we can determine the reality of the new birth.

Do not be too hard on yourself. Do not expect instant perfection. The very fact that you struggle against the evil within and without is an indication of spiritual life. Remember that Paul was an old man when he wrote the epistle to the Romans and he had to say, "I am not practicing what I would like to do" (Romans 7:15). He was even older when he wrote to the Philippians that he had not yet arrived, but was pressing toward the mark for the prize of his high calling (Philippians 3:13,14). The acid test is not how spiritual you are now, but how much progress you are making toward the goal. To use the modern idiom, hang in there.

Jesus called Simon Peter after the lesson in fishing and said, "Follow me." Discipleship is following Christ.

17

It is entering His school in Christian citizenship. He never teaches by exhortation. He always teaches by demonstration. He shows us how. He showed the disciples how to heal by healing. He showed them how to witness by witnessing. He showed them how to pray by praying. He showed them how to love by loving. He showed them how to suffer by suffering. You can learn, too, in His school. Life can begin again. Follow Him.

John Oxenham caught the Spirit of Christ's call to us in the following words:

"Who answers Christ's insistent call
Must give himself, his life, his all,
Without one backward look.
Who sets his hand unto the plow
And glances back with anxious brow,
His calling hath mistook.
Christ claims him wholly for His own;
He must be Christ's and Christ's alone."

Will It Last?

"Suppose life begins again for me—can it really last? Will I go back to the same old fear, frustration and failure?" Why don't we ask Peter? He is now an old man. He has spent a lifetime since that day on the beach, since he met Jesus Christ. He writes his first epistle as an old man, an apostle of Jesus Christ. He has followed Jesus Christ across many years. The Savior was crucified years ago and he writes to "the aliens who are chosen." They are aliens in a strange land who are "citizens of heaven." He says, "Blessed be the God and Father of our Lord Jesus Christ, who according to His great mercy has caused us to be born

18

again to a living hope through the resurrection of Jesus Christ from the dead, to obtain an inheritance which is imperishable and undefiled and will not fade away, reserved in heaven for you, who are protected by the power of God through faith for a salvation ready to be revealed in the last time" (I Peter 1:3-5 NASB). He says that the new birth we have experienced brings us into an inheritance which is "imperishable." It cannot "fade away." It is reserved for us against that day of Christ's return. It is "protected by the power of God."

At the wedding in Cana of Galilee, when Jesus turns the water into wine, the host serves the miraculous wine and the guests say, "You have saved the best wine until last" (John 2:10). This is very true of His miracle of new birth. It gets better. But it is never true when one serves the gods of this world. When you serve the gods who are not gods and come to the time when payment is due, they are always bankrupt and cannot pay. There is pleasure in sin "for a season," but it never lasts. Our Lord saves the best wine until last. Growing old spiritually is rather as Robert Browning pictured growing old physically:

> *Grow old along with me! the best is yet to be,*
> *The last of life, For which the first was made.*

As someone once said, "The Devil has no happy old men."

The Sermon on the Mount is all about lasting happiness. Happiness is a pure heart. Happiness is a gentle spirit. Happiness is being merciful. Happiness is the ability to be sad over the things that hurt others. It is a lasting happiness.

Christ gives us life that cannot be terminated; a peace that cannot be disturbed; a righteousness that cannot be tarnished; a love that cannot be diminished. He gives us eternal life. He says that He gives us peace

19

"not as the world gives peace." His peace does not come in a bottle or a hypodermic needle. His love does not come in an unholy relationship. His righteousness does not come masked in a hypocritical smile. His life is not measured in acres of land or number of shares or bank balances. All of these things are fading and transitory. "Our inheritance," says Peter, "cannot fade away."

A Royal Air Force pilot, returning from a mission over the English Channel, in what Churchill called "England's finest hour" during the Second World War, decided to go to his little village church on the channel coast for a Sunday morning service. When he got to the little village, he found it in ruins from a Luftwaffe raid the previous week. He parked his jeep and began walking through the village, which was deserted. From the direction of the bombed-out hulk of the village church, he heard singing, and he made his way to it. The villagers had cleared out the rubble of broken pews and furniture and, gathered within the remnants of the walls still standing, they were singing:

Change and decay in all around I see;
O Thou, who changest not, abide with me! ...
Hold Thou Thy cross before my closing eyes;
Shine through the gloom and point me to the skies;
Heaven's morning breaks, and earth's vain shadows flee;
In life, in death, O Lord, abide with me!

Yes, dear heart, it will last. By the new birth, you receive God's kind of life. The life that can begin again for you at this moment is life from God. His life does not depend on what you possess (Luke 12:15). It is more than something to eat (Luke 12:23). "These things Jesus said, and then looked up to God and said to Him, 'Father, the time has come, glorify Your Son, that the Son may glorify You. You gave Him authority over all men, so that He could give eternal life to all that You have given Him. Eternal life is knowing You, the only true God, and Jesus Christ whom You sent' " (John 17:13). The new life in Christ rests on His promise. Believe Him. Receive Him. Life can begin again.

I don't understand what's going on with me. I have everything. I made it all myself. Is Mary finally getting to me? It's like I'm hungry all the time, an empty feeling inside. Maybe I ought to see a doctor. I'm strong as a horse. I don't need a doctor. Mary says I need God. What do I need Him for? This office building—it's really plush. I did it all myself. That factory out there— God, how I love it. It's my life. There are fifty men out in the field today. They've all got good jobs. I gave them everything they've got. I did it all.

There is one thing I didn't do. I didn't make Mary as good and beautiful as she is. If there is a God, He did that. God, how I love that woman. Two weeks ago, when I thought I might lose her, man, I was crazy. The pastor prayed and asked God to take care of her. He did take care of her. I thank Him for that. God, I thank you. I did it—I just prayed. That's the first time I ever did it.

Mary keeps talking about being born again. Man, I can't understand stuff like that. I opened her Bible that night when I was alone in the house. Right there on one of the blank pages in the back was, "Charles is so good, Father. I want him to be a Christian. Send your Holy Spirit to him and convince him that he is a sinner and needs a Savior." I wonder if that's what is wrong with me. Is the Holy Spirit working on me?

2.

THE WIND OF THE SPIRIT

"Now there was a man of the Pharisees, named Nicodemus, a ruler of the Jews; this man came to Him by night, and said to Him, 'Rabbi, we know that You have come from God as a teacher; for no one can do these signs that You do unless God is with him.'

"Jesus answered and said to him, 'Truly, truly, I say to you, unless one is born again, he cannot see the kingdom of God.'

"Nicodemus said to Him, 'How can a man be born when he is old? He cannot enter a second time into his mother's womb and be born, can he?'

"Jesus answered, 'Truly, truly, I say to you, unless one is born of water and the Spirit, he cannot enter into the kingdom of God. That which is born of the flesh is flesh; and that which is born of the Spirit is spirit. Do not marvel that I said to you, "You must be born again." The wind blows where it wishes and you hear the sound of it, but do not know where it comes from and where it is going; so is everyone who is born of the Spirit.'

"Nicodemus answered and said to Him, 'How can these things be?'

"Jesus answered and said to him, 'Are you the teacher of Israel, and do not understand these things? Truly, truly, I say to you, we speak that which we know, and bear witness of that which we have seen; and you do not receive our witness. If I told you earthly things and you do not believe, how shall you believe if I tell you heavenly things?' " (John 3:1-12 NASB).

"Jesus Christ must die." So decided the Sanhedrin, the convocation of the religious aristocracy that ruled the capitol, Jerusalem. He preferred fishermen to the aristocracy. He loved children more than Pharisees and the poor more than scribes. He had offended the Altar, the Bank and the Academy. He was not good for business.

Jesus had gone to the Holy City for the Feast of Tabernacles. Jesus had made claim to a relationship with God. He had done miracles. Many of the people were saying, "This is the prophet."

The aristocratic Sanhedrin had a meeting. The priests represented the Altar, jealous for the crowds coming to the temple who gave them their power and their money. The scribes represented the Academy, responsible for maintaining the power of the priests over the people through a system of endless laws and musty traditions. The elders came to the meeting. They represented the bank, the moneyed class. Their consensus was that Jesus Christ must die.

Only one voice was raised in protest (John 7:45-52). Most Bible students fail to give Nicodemus proper credit for the protest, "Our law does not find a man guilty without hearing his testimony. Does this body really know what it is doing?" True, there was no vehement denunciation of the awful crime they were about to commit; there was no passionate declaration, "If you kill Him, kill me too." Still, Nicodemus was not the

24

same as the others. He was different. He had been changed.

In the fading daylight of that first Good Friday, we meet Nicodemus again. Joseph had received permission to take care of the body of Jesus and we see him going to the Hill of the Skull with a white winding sheet and linen bands over his arm. On the way, he is met by Nicodemus, whose servants bear a heavy load of myrrh and aloes.

They struggle as they pull the nails from His hands and feet and then bear the body torn by seven gaping wounds to a garden with a sepulcher owned by Joseph of Arimathea. The two rich men prepare the friend of the poor for burial. They carefully wash the body covered with a mixture of sweat and dust and blood. They fill the deep black wounds with the precious ointment and the fragrant spices. They kiss His forehead and recite the psalm of death and carefully wrap the body from head to toe. They place the body in the cave-tomb and close the opening with one great stone and leave. They could not know that, in three days, the grave clothes in which they had so carefully wrapped Him would be lying unoccupied just as they had wound them around Him.

Nicodemus said all he could in the meeting of the Sanhedrin and he did all he could after the crucifixion. He has been the object of scorn because, in the meeting of the Sanhedrin, the question was asked, "No one of the rulers or Pharisees has believed in Him, has he?" (John 7:48 NASB). This question was probably thrown out as a trap because of the rumors concerning the visit of Nicodemus to Jesus by night. Nicodemus never answered that question. There are times when silence is wiser than words. Another barb was probably thrown at Nicodemus in that same meeting. After Nicodemus raised his question about the legality of the proceedings, the question was again thrown directly to him, "You are not also from Galilee, are you?"

25

(John 7:52). In spite of his silence, he was not the same as the rest. Sometimes there is more courage in silence than there is in rash words. Something good happened to Nicodemus that night in Jerusalem when he visited the Galilean. His heart had been radically changed. He was a new creation.

Nicodemus came to Jesus because he had a need. He did not need money. Only a wealthy man could have brought a mixture of myrrh and aloes that weighed over one hundred pounds (John 19:39).

He did not need religion. There were only about six thousand Pharisees and they all took a pledge to obey every Scribal law. This was not only the law in the Old Testament. On the laws concerning the Sabbath, there are only a few words in the Scriptures, but, in the oral traditions of the time as later compiled in the Mishnah (a collection of decisions of the rabbis), there are twenty-four chapters on the Sabbath. If that is not enough, there are sixty-four columns in the Jerusalem Talmud (the codification of Jewish law and tradition). All of this he meticulously and carefully observed to the smallest detail. There were hundreds of other major areas whose codified laws ran to even greater length.

He did not need power because he was a member of the Sanhedrin, the ruling aristocracy. He may have been a member of a very distinguished family that can be traced back to 63 B.C. when a certain Nicodemus was sent by Aristobulus as an ambassador to Pompey, the Roman Emperor.

He had heard of the miracles done by Jesus of Nazareth. Was this man a word from the Beyond? Was this another cheap charlatan preying on gullible people? The only concession that Nicodemus made to Jesus when they met at night was, "You must be a teacher come from God because no one could do the miracles you are doing unless God is with him" (John 3:2). He had heard about the kind of miracles Jesus

26

performed—healing, ministering miracles—bread for the hungry, life for the dead, health for the sick. They were not the cheap tricks that helped no one and elicited coins from the pleased onlookers. There was no sleeping on a bed of nails or sticking a knife through the folds of skin in order to hear the crowd gasp.

"God must be with this man," thought Nicodemus. But, because he was a Pharisee and a member of the Sanhedrin, he had to be careful. He found out where Jesus was staying and came to Him at night. Quite often, in the houses of that time, the guest room was apart from the rest of the home, with a private entrance. There was in Nicodemus a hunger for something more than voluminous laws for keeping the Sabbath—more than endless rules and regulations. The Galilean might give him some light or tell him something—something that would satisfy his search for meaning.

It is difficult for us to see Nicodemus as an intellectual because he is so religious. There had been no breakthrough of the supernatural in his life. Though the reasoning of the Pharisees regarding the law was often faulty and illogical, the law was the law—it was cut and dried, memorized, accepted. When Jesus does not discuss the miracles He is doing, but says, "Unless one is born again, he cannot see the Kingdom of God," Nicodemus is suddenly faced with the supernatural. He can only question, "How can a man be born when he is old?"

Nicodemus was attracted by the humanitarian ideas of Jesus—that was the nature of the Galilean's miracles. There are thousands who like and applaud the humanitarian ideas of the church. Christians have always been very interested in this world. It was Christians who initiated prison reform, better treatment for labor in England and America, and the emancipation of slaves. But, for the humanist, any belief in the supernatural or afterlife is primitive superstition and such beliefs are considered psychological projections. This religious humanism is what masquerades as Christianity in many places. Many persons who attend and support the church have at best a very flimsy hold on a belief in the supernatural. Yet, without this belief, we are not Christians at all. In the sixties, this secular Christianity resulted in sex without love and murder without hate. The so-called secular church has no moorings, no faith and no future.

What does Jesus say to this intellectual—this humanist? Does He explain that, unlike other miracle workers, He only does miracles for teaching or healing? Does He expound the classic "proofs" for the existence of God? Does He lay on Nicodemus more rules and more burdens? Does He go to musty old volumes for a word from the ancients? He does none of these things. He goes straight to the need of Nicodemus:

"Nicodemus, you need new life. You need new eyes to see, new ears to hear, and a new tongue to taste the Kingdom of God. Nicodemus, there is a whole new world out there, a world you have never seen. It is God's world—the world I intended to be the Kingdom of God. It is a world just as real as this one, Nicodemus. God is not in ancient books and musty traditions, Nicodemus, He is here now. But, to see Him and know Him, you must be born again. Man has to be born of water and the Spirit. You were born of water the first time, a birth of the flesh. You must be born again of the Spirit. It is like the wind, Nicodemus. You see what the wind does, and because you do, you believe in the wind. Yet, you have never seen the wind. Nicodemus, I am talking about something I know. I am talking about something I have seen. This, Nicodemus, is your need. You should be able to understand that because you, as a master of Israel, should know what the prophets said about receiving a 'new heart' for the 'heart of stone' that our sins have given us. Nicodemus,

28

can't you feel the wind of the Spirit blowing now on your life?"

So many of us are caught in the trap of our own senses. The only things that are real to us are the things we can see or hear or taste or touch. "Some good blue chip stocks—now, I can believe in them. They are sure to increase in value. Land—I can put my trust in land because anyone knows there is only so much land. Steak and bread on the table—I can believe in them because I can smell and taste them. But who can put faith in an unseen kingdom? Who can believe in a King now dead two thousand years? Churches are all right because they make better communities and preserve our culture. But don't talk to me about life after death or being born again. It's spooky, man. I just don't believe. I'll put my faith in things that are real."

If we do not talk like that, isn't it true that we live like that? Isaac Watts describes us all too well:

> There are a number of us who creep
> Into the world to eat and sleep
> And know no reason why we're born,
> But only to consume the corn,
> Devour the cattle, flesh, and fish,
> And leave behind an empty dish.
> And if our tombstone when we die,
> Be not taught to flatter and to lie
> There is nothing better can be said,
> Than that he's eaten up all his bread,
> Drunk up his drink and gone to bed.

"The just shall live by faith." Martin Luther found this verse of Scripture and in it he found liberation and new life. We do not live by touch, taste, smell and sight. This is what Jesus is saying to Nicodemus. In the wilderness, Jesus Christ said to the Tempter who came to Him and offered Him bread in exchange for a selfish miracle, "Man shall not live by bread alone." Jesus was hungry, but He refused to perform the miracle and reminded the Tempter that man is more than an animal.

It is this spiritual life of man that is dead because of sin. It can only be made alive in a resurrection that is called, in Scripture, the new birth. It is difficult to tell in John 3 where the conversation with Nicodemus ends, but there is no reason to believe that John 3:16 was not a part of the conversation. Jesus makes it clear that only those who believe in Him will have eternal life. "And there is salvation is no one else; for there is no other name under heaven that has been given among men, by which we must be saved" (Acts 4:12 NASB). The just shall live by faith and not by sight or sound or taste or touch.

The Explanation of a Great Mystery

Jesus first said to Nicodemus, "Unless one is born again, he cannot see the Kingdom of God." Jesus was saying, "Nicodemus, you have been searching for that word from the Beyond. But this is not a word you hear with your physical ears. The Kingdom of God is not seen with your physical eyes. You have physical ears and eyes but what you really need is spiritual ears and eyes."

This solves one of the great mysteries and stumbling blocks for the person who is sincerely seeking God. There are voices on both sides. One says that there is God and I know Him. Others say there is no God and, with all my seeking, I have never been able to find Him. While a young pastor in St. Louis, I enrolled in a great university in that city. I took a course in geology. We had one professor for lectures and another for laboratory work. The lecture professor was a devout Christian who constantly shared his faith in Christ. He saw the "Rock of Ages" in every rock. He saw the Ageless One in all the geological ages of the earth. The laboratory professor was an unbeliever who saw man as an "accident of evolution." He ridiculed faith in God as a contradiction to the testimony of geology. Both were trained in the same science. How do you explain that?

Another example of this conflicting testimony was the contrast between the testimony of the first Russian cosmonaut and the first American astronaut. The Russian went into earth orbit, returned and said, "I saw no heaven. I saw no God. There is no heaven, no God."

The American returned from his orbit and said, in a testimony given in a church a few weeks later, "I saw God in space." In the words of the hymn of airmen, he said he "reached out and touched the face of God."

Both men were trained observers of phenomena. Both men were cool men of science. Did one of them lie and the other tell the truth? No, they both "told it like it was." How do you explain the difference? I cannot, but Jesus did. He said, "Unless one is born again he cannot see the Kingdom of God." In the words of a popular TV character, "That's the name of that story."

A rose, however fragrant, is never appreciated by someone who has no sense of smell. A magnificent symphony played by the most accomplished musicians cannot be enjoyed by one who has no sense of hearing. A sunset, no matter how gorgeous, is never appreciated by someone who has no sense of sight. A baby's skin, no matter how soft and smooth, is never appreciated by someone who has no sense of touch. A superb dessert, no matter how delicious, is never appreciated by someone who has no sense of taste. The five senses are the gift of the Creator by which we appreciate the

31

world around us—the world of nature. There are spiritual senses which, when awakened from death by the wind of the Spirit, give us the capability of knowing and understanding the world of the spiritual—the Kingdom of God.

One can walk right by God and never see Him. One can live right beside a miracle and never know it. I love the lyrics that sing,

> Every time you see a rose,
> Aren't you glad you got a nose?

I am so grateful for the gift of spiritual hearing and sight that make me *know* He lives. I cannot see Him with physical eyes, but He is here. I cannot hear Him with physical ears, but He speaks to me. The fragrance of His presence only comes to those whose spiritual senses are made alive. I'm glad I have a spiritual "nose."

Often men of science or learning who have made some great discovery are quoted as not believing in the supernatural. Some Christians are disturbed by this. I am not. It simply means that the person has no capacity for the spiritual. Because a man is an authority on something does not make him an authority on everything. If my wife is sick, I do not take her to an automobile mechanic. Someone suggested humorously, "If the baby swallows a nickel, you do not call the Collector of Internal Revenue." If I want an opinion about God, I want to find someone who has had an experience with God—who knows Him experientially. The expert may be learned or unlearned. He may be a blue collar worker or an executive. If I want knowledge about God, I want to go to someone who has had experience with God. Nicodemus went to the right person. He went to the One who is God, who came from God, who could say that He knew the Father (John 1:1-3).

You Must Be Born Again

Dwight L. Moody, the great evangelist, was once asked, "Mr. Moody, why do you preach so much that you must be born again?"

Mr. Moody replied, "Because you must be born again."

There are many things one can do without. Education is extremely valuable and I do not want what I am about to say to be taken as an endorsement of failing to get an education when one is available but one can do well without education. An immigrant arrived in the United States and applied for a job as a custodian. When it was found that he could not read, he was not employed. The immigrant made a pushcart, mounted a popcorn popper on it and started selling popcorn in the streets. One thing led to another until he was known as the Popcorn King of America.

Now a very wealthy man, he was interviewed by a reporter for a human-interest story. After a great deal of conversation, the reporter said, "Is it true that you could not read when you came to this country?"

The immigrant replied, "It is true, and to this day I can read very little."

The reporter observed, "Just think of what you might have been if you had been able to read."

The Popcorn King answered, "Yes, if I had been able to read, I would have been the custodian in that building."

You can do without health. Edward Gibbon, the great historian whose *Decline and Fall of the Roman Empire* is a classic, never knew a day of good health from his youth until he died at a very early age.

You can do without physical freedom. Prisons have

given us Paul's letters, *Pilgrim's Progress, Imitation of Christ,* and Dietrich Bonhoeffer's *Letters and Papers from Prison,* to mention only a few of the many works that have on them the smell of prison damp.

You can do without wealth. Some of the happiest and most well adjusted persons have very little in the way of possessions. But *you must be born again.*

You can travel widely and see all the world's great cities, but, if you have not been born again, you will never see the Holy City, New Jerusalem.

You may eat in the finest restaurants in the world, but, if you have never been born again, you will never sit down with Him to eat "the marriage supper of the Lamb."

You may see all the great trees of the world, the cedars of Lebanon, the lindens of New Zealand, and the sequoias of California, but if you have never been born again you will never see the Tree of Life. *You must be born again.*

We do not need simply a refurbishing at some minor point in our existence. Jesus did not say to Nicodemus, "You have made a good beginning, Nicodemus, because you are calling me a 'teacher.' Now, all you need is to begin from that point with some minor corrections in your thinking." Jesus insisted on a radical change of direction for Nicodemus. It was so radical a departure that Nicodemus had difficulty grasping the concept. Nicodemus did not need a cure, he needed a resurrection. He did not need a new attitude. He needed a new life. Jesus never once appealed to any goodness or evil in the nature of Nicodemus in order to build on that. Jesus never suggests that all we need is a completion of "that spark of divinity already in us." He demands a new beginning, a new life, a new birth. He is interested in creating a "new man."

Paul carries this thought into the existence of the church when he refers to the church as "a new race of man." The new birth is a *radical* change in man because it intends to change man at the very root (Latin *radix*) of his existence. It is a new creation. "Therefore if any man is in Christ, he is a new creature; the old things passed away; behold, new things have come" (II Corinthians 5:17 NASB). This creation is so new that it is, in essence, God's work of art. "For we are His workmanship, created in Christ Jesus for good works, which God prepared beforehand, that we should walk in them" (Ephesians 2:10 NASB).

The Answer Is Blowin' in the Wind

Bob Dylan, one of the poets of protest in the 1960s who has had a renewal of popularity in the 1970s, looked at some of the problems we were having at that time. He sang about the struggles of a young man for identity, the agony of Vietnam, the heartbreak of a marriage on the rocks. While some other singers were asking, "Who will answer," Dylan was singing, "The answer is blowin' in the wind."

Isn't this exactly what Jesus said to Nicodemus? "The wind blows where it wants to, and you hear the sound it makes. You do not understand the mystery of the wind. You believe that there is such a thing as the wind, and you see what it can do. This is true also of everyone who is born of the Spirit" (John 3:8).

Nicodemus had been driven back to another insistent question: "The new birth, Jesus, about which you speak. I grant it may be possible. But how does it take place?"

The answer of Jesus revolves around the fact that both the Greek and the Hebrew words for "spirit" have two meanings. The word may mean either "spirit" or "wind." The Greek word is *pneuma* and the Hebrew word is *ruach*. Just substitute the word "spirit" for "wind" in the answer of Jesus and you have His illustration that must have been clear to a student of the

35

Hebrew Scriptures such as Nicodemus. "The *Spirit* works where He wants to. You see what the *Spirit* does, but you do not understand all the mysteries of how He works. When He comes into your life, you will know what He has done, but you still will not understand all the mystery of how He does it."

The airlines would very much like to understand all the mysteries of the wind. One recent airline crash was blamed on a wind sheer. Clear-air turbulence is not yet understood. But it is there and it is a fact that the airlines must live with. We very much believe in the wind as one of the forces of nature. The wind, whose touch can be as soft as a gentle zephyr and as devastating as a tornado, is very much a part of our lives.

The Holy Spirit, the third person of the Triunity of God, is God working in human lives. As God, He is sovercign and works "where He wants to." We are not born of "the will of man" but of God. The Holy Spirit convicts us of our sin of not believing in Jesus Christ. "And He [The Holy Spirit], when He comes, will convict the world concerning sin. . . . concerning sin, because they do not believe in Me" (John 16:8,9 NASB). The Holy Spirit will remind us of what Jesus said: "But the Helper, the Holy Spirit, whom the Father will send in My name, He will teach you all things, arid bring to your remembrance all that I said to you" (John 14:26 NASB). The world will not be able to seize and crucify the Holy Spirit as it did Jesus. "That is the Spirit of Truth whom the world cannot seize (arrest), because it cannot see Him or know Him, but you know Him because He lives in you" (John 14:17). The Holy Spirit convinces us of our sinful rejection of Jesus Christ. He shows us the promises of Jesus Christ in regard to eternal life. He controls our lives after we are born again and assists us in living a Christian life. "For all who are being led (controlled) by the Spirit of God, these are the sons of God" (Romans 8:14).

The wind of the Spirit blew across the life of a drunken ballplayer of the Chicago White Stockings team and he was born again to be one of the great evangelists and fighters for social justice in American history, Billy Sunday. The wind of the Spirit blew across New York City in 1838 and what religious historians came to call the "Year of Miracle" brought new life to thousands and a new start for the nation. The answer is really blowin' in the wind.

There is for all our agonies, both personal and social, the wind of the Spirit. How many of us are living in our own private "hells" that we have created for ourselves? How many of us are feeling all boxed into a marriage that we do not want or a job that leaves us unfulfilled? I can hear you saying, "Aren't you really guilty of oversimplification? Aren't you really guilty of giving easy answers for very difficult and complicated questions?"

The answer I am giving is simple, but it is not easy. It is never easy for us to face ourselves, admit our sin and invite the help of God. It is never easy for us even to step on the threshold of faith, let alone to go through the door. It is never easy for us to exercise our will to step into the unknown and unseen. It is for this very reason that Jesus said, "For the gate is small, and the way is narrow that leads to life, and few are those who find it" (Matthew 7:14 NASB). Take that little bit of faith you have and, crying out, "I do believe; help me in my unbelief" (Mark 9:24 NASB), reach out to Jesus Christ and He will come to you.

It Happened to Me

Jesus said to Nicodemus, "What I am saying to you, Nicodemus, is true. It is true because it is something that we have seen and heard and experienced. I have

37

tried, Nicodemus, to tell you by using simple everyday experiences that you do not seem to understand. If you do not understand these earthly experiences, how can you understand spiritual experiences?"

It is important to understand intellectually and to be able to defend our faith, but it is far more basic and important to experience it. Many are shut out of the Kingdom of God because they want to understand first and then experience. How do we learn about the world around us? The answer is experience. Everything we really know, we know by experience. Many things we know by experience work, but we do not know why.

A case in point is a visit to a competent doctor, in whom we have confidence. He examines, diagnoses and then may prescribe drugs or treatments or surgery or a combination of these three. We do not understand a lot about the course he recommends. Only experience will determine if the doctor was correct. We trust him, we do what he says and, happily, we get better. There is no way a lay person can really understand what he has done. We believed in him and put ourselves in his hands. We can say, "I don't know what he gave me, but it worked."

Faith that is separated from experience in its inception is not likely to be related to experience in daily living. Cold creeds and dull dogmas affect life very little.

American society probably has not changed much since 1949 when ninety-five percent of the American people in a nation-wide poll said, "Yes, I believe in God." Only twenty-five percent said they tried to lead a good life as a consequence of their faith. Fifty-four per cent said religion did not affect their politics or their business.

In contrast to this obvious divorce of faith and experience, Jesus placed great emphasis on how a person lives. His idea of the final judgment in Matthew 25 is revealing. The final test is not orthodoxy but living in right relationship to our fellow human beings. In the parable of the good Samaritan, "eternal life" is directly related to one's love for his neighbor. A neighbor is defined as anyone of our fellow men who is in trouble (Luke 10:25-36).

Is God for real with you? Do you know Jesus Christ as your own personal Savior? Is your experience with Jesus Christ life renewing? Too often our knowledge is about a theoretical God. We know about Jesus Christ and believe the facts, even the supernatural facts, of His life. But we do not know Him personally.

Someone might ask me, "Do you know Jimmy Carter, President of the United States?"

I would say, "Of course I know him. He was Governor of Georgia. His wife is Rosalynn. His daughter is Amy. He has a son named Chip. He is a born again Christian."

"But," they say, "do you know him personally?"

I have to say, "No, I don't know him personally."

Then imagine that the President writes me and invites me to visit with him in Washington for a week. I stay in the White House. We have breakfast together. We pray together. We share experiences. After a week with him, I return home. Then someone asks me, "Do you know Jimmy Carter."

My face brightens and I say, "Sure I know him personally."

Do you know Jesus Christ personally?

God So Loved the World

It is not easy to tell if John 3:16 is in the words of John or Jesus. Because John is speaking for God, however, it really makes no difference. The promise is that God will give eternal life through a new birth to those who "believe in Jesus Christ."

This means that we believe God is just as Jesus says He is. God loves us. He cares about us. He is a loving Father. He wants to forgive us, cleanse us and save us from ourselves and our sins. It also means that we believe Jesus is all that God said Him to be. "And after being baptized, Jesus went up immediately from the water; and behold, the heavens were opened, and He saw the Spirit of God descending as a dove, and coming upon Him, and behold, a voice out of the heavens, saying, 'This is My beloved Son, in whom I am well pleased.' " (Matthew 3:16,17 NASB). "And the Word became flesh, and dwelt among us, and we beheld His glory, glory as of the only begotten from the Father, full of grace and truth" (John 1:14 NASB).

Sir Walter Scott, in his *Heart of Midlothian,* tells a beautiful story about Jeannie Deans. Her sister has gotten into trouble in London and is condemned to die. Jeannie is determined to go to London and plead personally with the queen to spare the life of her sister. A touching scene takes place when Reuben Butler, a school teacher, tries to stop her from going. He tells her that the road to London is dangerous and he reminds her that she is a woman and will be alone. He tells her about the highwaymen who may rob and kill her. He ends his argument by saying, "Why don't you write a letter?"

Jeannie answers. "Writing wouldna' do it. A letter canna look and pray and beg and beseech as a human voice can do to a human heart. A letter's like the music that the ladies have for their spinets—nothing but black scores compared with the same tune played and sung. The word of mouth maun do it or naething else."

God did not send a letter to plead with you and me. He sent His Son. In a human voice He says to human hearts, "I came that you might have life, abundant

40

life, new life." A loving Father, God loved so much He gave His Son that we may have life. He comes to us at the point of our deepest need and makes His offer to us. His offer of life must be received by faith. My heart goes out to Him. My soul reaches up to Him. In Him I have life.

The Meaning of the Cross

Nicodemus would remember those words, "As Moses lifted up the serpent in the wilderness, even so must the Son of Man be lifted up."

Every person who is born of God must take at least one trip to Calvary with the Holy Spirit as his "Tour Guide." In not many months, Nicodemus, laden with linen cloths and spices, would assist Joseph of Arimathea in taking what was left from man's inhumanity, washing it, and wrapping it in the fine linen wrappings. He would kiss that face cold in death and twisted by suffering. He would chant the litany of death and seal the tomb with a large rock. Then he would know what the Son of God meant when He said, "The Son of Man must be lifted up."

Jesus had taught them over and over that there is no life without death, there is no birth without death. "The hour has come for the Son of Man to be glorified. Truly, truly, I say to you, unless a grain of wheat falls into the earth and dies, it remains by itself alone; but if it dies, it bears much fruit. He who loves his life loses it; and he who hates his life in this world shall keep it to life eternal" (John 12:23-25 NASB). Peter had recoiled against the teaching that Jesus must die in Jerusalem. Jesus told Peter that talking about His not dying on a cross was to talk like a devil and not a friend (Matthew 16:21-23).

41

The Holy Spirit always takes us to Calvary in His work of "convincing us of sin." He brings us into that scene of horror. We see the soldiers gambling for His clothing. Having finished their game, they sit down and watch Him die. They keep away the wild dogs eager to tear out his bowels and eat Him alive. The four-legged dogs, the authors of inquisition, hurl sputum and torments in his face. We hear them say, "If you are the Son of God, come down from the cross."

We hear Him cry, "I thirst." The daughters of Jerusalem, whose work of mercy is to give a deadening drink to victims of crucifixion, offer Him the pain-killing drink, but He refuses. Our Tour Guide stands quietly while we see the last agonies of His torture-racked body and we hear Him cry, "Father, into your hands I put my Spirit." He is dead.

We turn to the Tour Guide and ask, "Who is He?"

The Tour Guide answers, "He is Jesus, the Christ, the Son of God, Savior of sinners and Lord of glory. He came into the world to die for sinners. He had to die to conquer death. He was born as no other man was ever born—born of a virgin. He lived as no other man ever lived—the Man for Others. He loved as no other man ever loved—dying for sinners like you. He is the God-man who came into the world to show us that God is a loving Father and not the cruel heartless judge men suppose God to be."

We ask the Tour Guide, "What crime did He commit?"

"No crime," the Tour Guide answers, "unless loving people is a crime; unless crying out against the cruelty and injustice of man to man is a crime; unless exposing the injustices of the rich and the hypocrisies of the religious is a crime. No, He never committed a crime. He was the most all-loving person who ever lived."

In our indignation, with every nerve crying out against this greatest of all man's crimes, we ask the

Tour Guide, "Who did this to Him, who was in charge?"

The Tour Guide turns to us with infinite sadness and says, "You did it—you, my children. It was for your sins He died."

Our Tour Guide is gone now but the impact of that visit to Calvary never leaves us. At the cross, we experience moral shock. We see the enormity of our crime on Calvary and know that we are the guilty ones. We feel His awful agonies and know that we nailed Him there. At the cross, we feel guilt and sorrow. We cannot escape the personal responsibility for His suffering. "He died for me." These are the words spelled out by the lexicon of Calvary. At the cross, we find forgiveness. We see that, in dying for our sin, paying the penalty for our crimes, He made forgiveness possible. We hear Him cry again from that cross, "Father, forgive them, they don't know what they are doing." John Newton put all the agony and ecstasy of the cross into the following words:

> I saw One hanging on a tree,
>   In agony and blood;
> He fixed His languid eyes on me,
>   As near His cross I stood.
>
> Sure, never till my latest breath,
>   Can I forget that look:
> It seemed to charge me with his death,
>   Tho' not a word He spoke.
> My conscience felt and owned the guilt,
>   And plunged me in despair;
> I saw my sins His blood had spilt
>   And helped to nail Him there.
> Alas I knew not what I did,
>   But now my tears are vain:
> Where shall my trembling soul be hid?
>   For I the Lord have slain.

A second look He gave which said,
  "I freely all forgive:
This blood is for thy ransom paid,
  I died that thous may'st live.

A young nobleman, Count Nikolaus Ludwig von Zinzendorf, stood before the painting of the Crucifixion by Domenia Seti and wept. It was Zinzendorf's band of born again believers from which the Peter Bohler came who asked John Wesley the question, "Have you been born again?" When Wesley settled that question at Aldersgate, a series of spiritual events began which climaxed in the greatest revival of religion that the world has known, one that shook two continents. The power of that cross brought about a new birth of religious faith and enthusiasm in America. All denominations reaped the harvest of that spiritual awakening of experiential faith in Jesus Christ.

You can invite the Tour Guide to take you on a tour of Calvary. At the cross, you can experience a new birth. When the "wind of the Spirit" blows across your life, Jesus Christ can live and die before your spiritual eyes. The history of human guilt is climaxed in the cross. The purposes of God's love are made clear at the cross. The mysteries of prophecy are unraveled at the cross. The problem of human salvation is solved at the cross. The door to eternal life is opened at the cross. Hallelujah for the cross!

The spiritual asks, "Were you there when they crucified my Lord?" Once having been there with the Tour Guide, you can never be the same. The transforming power of the cross is the same "yesterday, today, and forever." It is both death and life for all men. What you do with Jesus Christ acting on your behalf on the cross will determine whether you are "in the process of destruction" or "in the process of salvation."

"For the Word of the cross is to those who are in the process of destruction foolishness, but to those of us in the process of being saved it is the power of God" (I Corinthians 1:18). The new birth is a birth into "the process of being saved" that begins with spiritual birth and continues to glorification of the believer when He returns. Nicodemus knew what that uplifted serpent on the pole meant. He knew that all who looked upon the symbol of God's salvation lived and all who refused to look died. Look and live! William Cowper wrote the words we sing in church:

> Dear dying Lamb, Thy precious blood
>   Shall never lose its power
> Till all the ransomed church of God
>   Be saved to sin no more:
>
> E'er since by faith I saw the stream
>   Thy flowing wounds supply,
> Redeeming love has been my theme,
>   And shall be till I die."

I really hate myself. Hitting him was what was so bad. He really deserved it, talking to me the way he did, saying I never loved him. How could he say that? I have given that boy everything. I shouldn't have hit him. That look on his face, with all that long hair—it was like hitting Jesus Christ. He can't seem to remember who is feeding him and putting clothes on his back and sending him to school.

I love him. When he was about five or six, I taught him to fly a kite. I guess I really quit spending time with him. It's so hard when you have to work the way I do. All the promotions I have worked for were really for him. Why doesn't he realize it? He is always talking to his mother. He never talks to me about anything any more. He used to talk to me about everything. What happened?

I really am sorry I hit him. I shouldn't have done that. I remember what the preacher said a few weeks ago. He said parents who have rebellious children are learning what it's like to be God. He is our Father. God, I hope you are doing better than I am. Come to think of it, I have treated God a lot worse than Billy is treating me. That's something else to feel bad about.

God, I have never felt so mean in my life as I do now. What I saw in his eyes and Martha's eyes really got to me. I think I'll go in and tell Billy that I'm sorry and that I love him. I might just do that with you too, God, when I get through with Billy.

3.

THE NEED TO REPENT

"And He said, 'A certain man had two sons; and the younger of them said to his father, "Father, give me the share of the estate that falls to me." And he divided his wealth between them.

"'And not many days later, the younger son gathered everything together and went on a journey into a distant country, and there he squandered his estate with loose living. Now when he had spent everything, a severe famine occurred in that country, and he began to be in need. And he went and attached himself to one of the citizens of that country, and he sent him into his fields to feed swine. And he was longing to fill his stomach with the pods that the swine were eating, and no one was giving anything to him.

"'But when he came to his senses, he said, "How many of my father's hired men have more than enough bread, but I am dying here with hunger! I will get up and go to my father, and will say to him, "Father, I have sinned against heaven, and in your sight; I am no longer worthy to be called your son; make me as one of your hired men.'" And he got up and came to his father.

" 'But while he was still a long way off, his father saw him, and felt compassion for him, and ran and embraced him, and kissed him. And the son said to him, "Father, I have sinned against heaven and in your sight; I am no longer worthy to be called your son."

" 'But the father said to his slaves, "Quickly bring out the best robe and put it on him, and put a ring on his hand and sandals on his feet; and bring the fattened calf, kill it, and let us eat and be merry; for this son of mine was dead, and has come to life again; he was lost, and has been found." And they began to be merry' " (Luke 15:11-24 NASB).

God made the world round, so the farther away you get, the closer to home you come. Thomas Wolfe said, "You can't go home again," but you can, if it is coming home to God. The story of the waiting father is distilled truth. Jesus' disciples, about to depart on their mission, needed faith and for them it was a parable of faith. The faith they would preach and teach is about a loving Father who wants sinful men to come to Him. Jesus confirms their faith in that message by a simple story.

The publicans and sinners were also standing near to hear Him. They needed hope more than anything else. Religious people spurned and shunned them. They needed hope and this story was for them a story of hope.

In the crowd were the scribes and Pharisees. The Pharisees came with their legitimizers, the scribes, to trap Him. Their hearts were as cold as the money they loved and as worm-eaten as the ancient documents over which they argued daily. Jesus knew that lovelessness is hell and for them this was a story of love—the love of a waiting Father who longs for the return of the prodigal.

48

The story could be called "The Homecoming." It is as up-to-date as tomorrow morning's newspaper. For all persons of all time who need faith, hope or love, Jesus told this story. The story is about the hunger in the heart of God for the return of the sinner, and the hunger in the heart of the sinner for the return to God.

One cold Saturday evening twenty-five years ago, I was wrestling with Luke 15:11-24 trying desperately to prepare a sermon on "The Prodigal Son" for Sunday morning. I was rather irritated when a knock on my study door disturbed my frantic search for a sermon. I opened the door and John, one of the deacons, came in. I sat down behind my desk and said, "John, what can I do for you?"

John answered, "Preacher, you got to help me. We've got to go down to the police station right now. John Junior is in jail." Now, this was not the first time that John Junior had been in jail. I had helped to get him out of several escapades for his father's sake.

I was irritated at being interrupted and I told John rather impatiently, "John, the best thing you can do for him is leave him in jail. It may do him some good." When John didn't answer, I continued, "You remember the time you had saved up enough money to buy a better house? You remember John Junior got in a scrape and your new house went down the drain. You remember when you thought that you and your wife would take the first vacation you had had in years. John Junior got in trouble and you never took the trip. John, I'm telling you, leave him in jail. It will do him good."

I stopped then because I realized that John not only had tears in his eyes, but was sobbing. My heart felt for him and I went over to him and put my arm around him and hugged him and said, "Don't cry, John: God will take care of it."

Then words, as if wrung out of his heart, came to

49

his lips. "Preacher," he said, "you just don't understand. You don't have any children. He's my boy. I've got to go down there."

There was my sermon on Luke 15. It was not the story of a prodigal son at all. It was the story of the waiting father. I pulled my coat down and put it on and said, "Come on, John, let's go down to the jail and get John Junior out."

The next morning, I wasn't just preaching about a story in the New Testament; I was telling them something I had seen and heard and felt. I knew the waiting father was like the waiting Father. God said, "We've got to go down there," too.

Someone once said there is no cross in the story of the waiting father. It is there. It is in the heart of the Father. When the Civil War was going well for the Union, someone asked Lincoln, "How will you treat the states that have left the Union after the war?"

Mr. Lincoln replied, "I will treat them as if they had never left."

Every parent who has had a child run away from home knows that, in the joy and relief of reuniting, recriminations and accusations are forgotten. In a matter of six words, Jesus tells us that God is like a person and that He is a Father. During the sixties, in the Christian centers in Haight Ashbury in San Francisco or on Tenth and Peachtree in Atlanta, there were always the notices on the bulletin boards: "Dearest Debbie, If you see this, please come home. Daddy and I love you so much. We wait for you day and night. If you need money, let us know. Just call us or write us and tell us you are all right. We pray for you, Debbie, every night. Come home soon, please."

There are thousands who have had their hearts broken by a son or daughter and yet have never once thought that they have forsaken God and broken His heart. Isaiah the prophet had predicted that the Lord would come and save Jerusalem. He had said to tell

50

the daughter of Zion (Jerusalem) the good news that God was coming as Lord and He would bring with Him the people He had rescued, "the holy people of God," "the people the Lord has saved" (Isaiah 62:11,12). But the city that God loved and would never forsake did not receive the Lord when He came. He stood and looked back at the city that rejected Him and said, "O Jerusalem, Jerusalem, the city that kills the prophets and stones those sent to her! How often I wanted to gather your children together, just as a hen gathers her brood under her wings, and you would not have it!" (Luke 13:34 NASB).

The story, however, is not only about the love of the father who waited for the return of his son, but about the son who returns and the way he comes home again. He does not come home as he went away, with his heart full of rebellion and distrust. He returns convinced that what he did was wrong. There was really nothing wrong with wanting the inheritance, because the Jewish laws were clear. The father had no choice. The older son, by law, received two-thirds and the younger son one-third (Deuteronomy 21:17). Very often, the division was made before the death of the father so that management could be given to the older son. There is a strong possibility that this prospect prompted the idea of division of the estate in the younger son's head.

There may have been serious conflict between the self-righteous holier-than-thou older son and the rebellious younger son. What he wanted was really his by birthright, but the purposes for which he intended it were very wrong. It was not wrong for him to want the estate but it was wrong callously to demand it before the father thought this wise. There are two brothers in the story. One is a hypocrite and the other is a rebel. The hypocrite may have contributed to the rebellion of the younger son. There are some of us who rebel against God and choose to live far away from

Him. There are others of us who pretend to live close to Him but our hearts are far away. One wants the inheritance so he can throw it away. The other wants the inheritance for himself.

The younger son "did his thing" and, if we can believe the older brother, he threw his inheritance away on gambling and prostitutes. He really lived it up. He knew "you only go around once in life" and you've got to get "nothing but the best." But these things were not so wrong. He left his father, rejected his love and care, and tried to live without him. The point of the story is that, when he returned, he did not return just any old way. He didn't call his father collect from Taos, New Mexico, and say, "Hey, Dad, I need some more bread." He did not come home in a new Jaguar telling the father that he really made it big in Las Vegas. He came home with a new attitude. He had changed his mind about his father. He was homesick. He was even willing to risk hearing his older brother say, "I told you so," to get back home. Christina Rossetti has drawn a word picture of the prodigal's change:

> Does that lamp still burn in my Father's house
>   Which he kindled that night I went away?
> I turned once beneath the cedar boughs,
>   And marked it gleam with a golden ray;
>   Did he think to light me home some day?

> Hungry here with the crunching swine,
>   Hungry harvest have I to reap;
> In a dream I count my Father's kine,
>   I hear the tinkling bells of his sheep,
>   I watch his lambs that browse and leap.

> There is plenty of bread to home,
>   His servants have bread enough and to spare;
> The purple wine-fat froths with foam,

Oil and spices make sweet the air,
  While I perish hungry and bare.

Rich and blessed those servants, rather
  Than I who see not my Father's face!
I will arise and go to my Father:
  'Fallen from sonship, beggared of grace,
Grant me, Father, a servant's place.'

What Does It Mean to Be "Lost?"

It is meaningful that this story is a companion to two other stories about a "lost coin" and a "lost sheep." The coin was a lost object through no fault of its own. The sheep was lost, straying because it knew no better. The son was lost, willfully and in rebellion. One of the stories is included in the gospel of Matthew and immediately follows, "the Son of Man is come to save that which was lost" (Matthew 18:11-13). The three stories have increasing significance and only the third reveals the exact nature of God's concern for the lost. God cares as a loving Father for a son who has willfully rebelled and has put distance between himself and the Father. What better word is there to describe modern man. People are lost from the good and the holy. They are lost in the faceless masks of anonymity that haunt the concrete jungles of our cities. They are lost in the depersonalizing computer. They are lost in the agonies of alcoholism. They are lost in pornography, the last refuge of those frustrated in sex. They are lost in the trap of a loveless marriage. They are lost in the madhouse of hard drugs. They are lost in the sameness and boredom of "eat, work, sleep" day after endless day.

To be lost is to be separated from God. "But your

iniquities have made a separation between you and your God, and your sins have hid His face from you, so that He does not hear" (Isaiah 59:2 NASB). In verse 12 of that same chapter, Isaiah uses three words that indicate just what it is that has separated us from God. "For our transgressions are multiplied before Thee, and our sins testify against us; for our transgressions are with us, and we know our iniquities." "Transgression" is a clear violation of the law of God. God says, "You shall not bear false witness," and we lie. "Sin" is missing the mark or the purpose that God has for us. It is being less than what we can be. "Iniquity" relates to the acts of wrongdoing such as greed or adultery.

The son was away from the father in our story because his attitudes and his actions were wrong. If mother says to her eight-year-old son, "Now, don't take the cookies from this cookie jar. I have made them for a special reason. Here are some cookies for you, but do not eat these other cookies." Then the son eats all of his cookies and, while she is gone, he eats the ones she had made for a special purpose. That is "transgression."

If the child brings home some bad grades from school and father says, "Son, I really expected more of you because you are really capable of a lot better than that," that is "sin."

If the eight-year-old says, "I didn't take cookies from the cookie jar," although he has crumbs all over his face and even the dog is eating a cookie, that is "iniquity." It is a lie, one act of wrongdoing.

If a person commits adultery, that is "transgression," for the law says, "Thou shalt not commit adultery." If someone hits another person in anger, that is "iniquity." If someone is mean and small with a waitress in a restaurant or a stewardess on a plane, that is "sin," because the person is certainly capable of much better behavior.

54

It is so important to see that all of these are not just violations of some cold inexorable moral code handed down from a smoking mountain millenniums ago. They are a break in relations with the loving Father. It is the certainty of the Fatherhood of God that makes the return possible. "You can go home again." The Father is not going to look on coldly while sinners break themselves against the unyielding law. He is going to "seek and save that which is lost." God is actually moved to grief and sorrow because of our sin. Only the cross can measure how much He cares. No person who has challenged the truth of God's fatherly love ever felt so deeply as He the problem of sin and alienation. Jesus was sure of the Father's concern and love. This never caused Him to take an easy or light view of sin and what it does to human minds and lives. He alone drank that bitter cup of alienation from God in Gethsemane. Jesus, the God-man, knew what it meant to be separated from God for He experienced it there in Gethsemane and cried out of the horror of that alienation. Seven times He cried out from the cross and twice He is vividly revealed as the God-man who died there. He cried out once, "Father, forgive them, they don't know what they are doing." Again he cried out, "My God, my God, why have you forsaken me?" He knew what it meant to be away from God. Because of our sin and alienation, we are not able to comprehend what it means to be separated from God. Once, as God, He forgave those who hated Him. Once, as man, He voiced the separation from God that man caused and He suffered.

To be lost is not to know who or where you are. You may say, "I know who I am; I am John Smith" or "Mary Doe" or whoever. Do you know that you are a son of the Heavenly Father, that you are made in the image of God, that you are heir to all the riches of God? Do you know that life is more than food or drink or clothes to wear? Do you know that you are more than a mouth to stuff with food and water, more than a carcass to clothe?

At this point, the relationship of our discussion to the new birth is apparent. We need to be "refathered." The prodigal never knew his father even though they had lived in the same house. The older brother did not know him. To one, the father was a "mean old man" and, to the other, he was a "doddering old idiot." When the prodigal came home and asked to become a servant, it was as if a son had been born. Just as at the birth of a son there is a feast to celebrate, so, on this occasion, the father said, "This son of mine was lost and is found, was dead and is now alive. Let the feasting begin." There is celebration and feasting when the son is refathered.

The problem is that we really do not know what God is like. To some, He is a "crabby old man" who issues orders about how we are to live. To others, God is deaf, dumb and blind, and can be deceived and manipulated according to their will. Knowing God is a new birth; it is knowing Him as the loving Father.

Born Free

Do you give a young man his inheritance when you know by intuition and experience that he will throw it away? God never violates man's birthright of freedom. Men make slaves of men, but God makes a slave of no man. The father gives the young man his inheritance because it is his birthright. God does not violate man's freedom in the first or the second birth. People are not forced by physical birth into being a slave to the will of parents or of God. When people are born again, they are "born free." They are still free to say "yes" or "no" to God. It is sin, not God,

56

that enslaves men. If men are in bondage, it is because they are enslaved by some other man or they are slaves to their own sin. An epitaph on the grave of John Jack, a slave born in Africa, was inscribed by Daniel Bliss with the following words: "God wills us free, man wills us slaves, I will as God wills, God's will be done."

Slave owners in Jamaica and in the United States were very reluctant to have slaves hear the gospel, because it created in them a desire to be free. When one says that he does not want to become a Christian because he will lose his freedom, he does not understand the nature of the relationship between God and the believer. It is the relationship of a loving father and his child. "And because you are sons, God has sent forth the Spirit of His Son into our hearts crying, 'Abba [Papa or Daddy]! Father!' Therefore you are no longer a slave, but a son; and if a son, then an heir through God" (Galatians 4:6,7 NASB).

Some people may say, "You talk about a new birth. I don't want 'Thou shalt not do this' and 'Thou shalt do this.' I want to be free." A born again Christian is not a slave to any set of rules. "For you were called to freedom, brethren; only do not turn your freedom into an opportunity for the flesh, but through love serve one another. For the whole law is fulfilled in one word, in the statement, 'You shall love your neighbor as yourself' " (Galatians 5:13,14 NASB). If the new man in Christ serves Christ, he serves Him voluntarily. He is always free.

We are slaves to so many things. We are slaves to the corporation rat race. We are slaves to the American success syndrome. We are slaves to the hypodermic needle, pornography and a whole house full of plastic gods who are not gods. Modern man stands in bonds and shackles declaring all the time that he is free and will be a slave to no one. The Jewish leaders objected when Jesus promised them that they could be free if they had a right relationship with God. They said, "We are the children of Abraham and have never been slaves to anyone. Why are you saying to us, 'You can be free?' " At that very moment, they were in bondage to the Romans and before that they had been slaves in Egypt and Babylonia.

Man is utterly blind to the slavery in which he lives. Alcoholism, mental depression, psychosomatic conditions such as colitis, diverticulitis, hiatal hernia, ulcers, hypertension, and heart disease, are often symptoms of slavery to the constant lie that we are free when, all of the while, we are living in the worst kind of slavery. People need a "new birth" of freedom.

Do not lie to yourself about your present condition. It is never easy to face the truth about ourselves. Peter talks about people who claim to be free, who are really the slaves of their sin and guilt. "Speaking arrogant and vain words, they entice, by their sensuality, weak people who are barely escaping their lies, promising them freedom, and all the time they are the slaves of corruption, because whatever controls a man enslaves him" (II Peter 2:18,19). Jesus says to His disciples, "You shall know the truth and the truth shall make you free. . . . If the Son makes you free, you will really be free" (John 8:32,36). Kate Wilkins Woolley said it well in her hymn:

Free to be me, God, I really am free;
 Free to become what you want me to be;
Free to decide whether I should be lord,
 Or be your slave and obey your word.

Freedom, possession that makes me like you,
 Frightens me, God, when its meaning seeps through;
Blessing or curse, Lord, condemned to be free?
 Free, but responsible, free to be me.

Free to live fully, to follow your way,
  Give myself wholly, to die every day;
Free to be real, God, to strip off the mask,
  Be your creation, it's all that I ask.

God, in choosing to make people free, has given them the liberty to distrust and disobey Him. It is this risk that God takes in making people in His own image. We are not God's creation to be controlled by His omnipotence. We are also free to control ourselves by a voluntary and loving relationship with God as Father. We are free to obey God. The lack of freedom is possible in the creature-Creator relationship but not in the Father-child relationship. God wants to create a loving family for fellowship with Himself. He wants free people, not puppets.

For freedom to be real, there must be a choice. The prodigal must be free to leave home if he is to be free to return. People must be free to sin if they are free not to sin. Sin is our refusal to accept the Father's love and care. It is putting distance between us and God. Self-assertion is a part of that freedom. There is in all of us the need to express and assert our individuality. When the self-assertion becomes rebellion, it is sin. Self-will is a sin, but self-control is a virtue. Persons can sink to bestiality or rise to sainthood to the glory of God. When the Bible says, "For all have sinned and fallen short of the glory of God," (Romans 3:23) it means that all men since Adam have refused the Father's love and have gone their own way (Isaiah 53:6).

It is exactly at this point that there is hope. When a person goes his own way and feels it is really great, there is in that person a growing discontent and unrest. The prodigal begins to think more and more of home and Father. "It really wasn't that bad at home," he begins to think. There is a sense of need that he really cannot define, but it is there. As his money dwindles and his friends are gone, the feeling deepens. That feeling is a sense of dependence on the Father. This need for God is built into all of us. H. G. Wells called it "that God-shaped blank" that is in every man. Even Karl Marx admitted man is "incurably religious." Friedrich Schleiermacher, one of the world's greatest theologians, said that religion is a "sense of dependence."

We accumulate great wealth, but there is something missing. We attain great fame, but there is something missing. We bury ourselves in work or business or pleasure, but there is something missing. We try to stifle that feeling of dependence, that inner loneliness, and act as if we are the masters of our own fate. When we live like that, we are living in a phony Barnum and Bailey world. The very gifts that we have used to create our phony existence of wealth or power or sensual living are the gifts that were given to us by the Father.

What Is Sin?

The young man of our story must know the depths of his "lostness" before he will come home. He must come to know the meaning of the words "sin" and "judgment" and "punishment" before he can again enjoy the Father's house. Sin is both a possibility and an actuality. Before sin is an act, it is an attitude.

A very religious rich young man came to Jesus. He wanted very much to be a part of the "Jesus group." He said that he had kept all the commandments and had never broken one. Jesus reminded him that he lacked one thing, and pointed out the young man's love of money. It was not an act but an attitude that kept him from knowing the Father (Luke 18:18-24). Not all of us have the same sin-barrier that keeps us from knowing the Father. With Nicodemus (John 3), it was pride; with the woman of Samaria (John 4), it was prostituted sex; with the rich young man (Luke 18), it was the love of money.

None of these could experience a new birth until their sin was faced and forgiven. Two of the three found Christ in the experience of new birth and the third "went away sad, for he was very rich." He loved money more than he loved God. Jesus Christ confronted each of these people at the point of their sin and met them at the point of their need.

Jesus never uses "symptom therapy." He never meets us except at that point where something is radically wrong with us at the core of our being. He treats the disease, not the rash that is caused by the disease. The disease that needs healing is sin.

Sin is the misuse of the gifts of the Father. In a very real way, it is the goodness of God that makes sin possible. The Father, in His goodness, has given gifts to all of us by our first birth. These gifts are our talents. The gifts are a reflection of the person of God. An example is the power to create wealth. "But you shall remember the Lord your God, for it is He who is giving you the power to make wealth, that He may confirm His covenant which He swore to your fathers, as it is this day" (Deuteronomy 8:18). This is a gift of the Father, but it can be misused. God has given us the power to use or misuse our gifts. He gives us the gifts and the freedom to use or misuse them because He wants us to be free.

The animals are guided by instinct and the stars are guided by mathematical precision but people have mind that can think evil; they have wills that can do evil; they have hearts that can love evil. People can also think truth. They can will to do good. They can choose to love God and their fellowmen. The same gifts that can make a person bestial or self-centered can also make him loving and caring toward others. The power to create wealth, for example, can make a man a money-loving miser or a beneficent person who clears slums to erect decent housing for the poor. What is a human being? Is he a Jonas Salk or an Adolf Hitler? Is he the creator of charity hospitals or massage parlors? Does he write great books or pornography?

Jesus came into the world because human beings could not solve the riddle of their own existence. As Son of God, He came to show us what the Father is like. If we want to know the Father, we must know Him. This was His claim and challenge to humanity. He showed us how the Father had gifted us for life on this planet. As Son of Man, He showed us how those gifts can be used for the glory of the Father and the good of others. He shows us what we can be when we use the Father's gifts.

Among the gifts that He evidenced as a man was the gift of using the tools of a carpenter with skill to shape a yoke for an ox, for example. He magnified the gifts of the common man. Jesus showed us how we are misusing the Father's gifts. In coming to Christ, we are coming to the Father. In Him we are "refathered" or "born again." Then He shows us how to use the Father's gifts in ways we have never known. When people begin to use the gifts of the Father in right ways, children have "new fathers"; wives have "new husbands"; parents have "new children"; and society has "new citizens." He shows us how we can be "salt" and "light" and "leaven" in all the relationships of life.

The gifts that God has given people are misused both personally and socially. The gift of sex has been misused in adulterous relationships, homosexuality and pornography. The gift of healing has been withheld from the poor and misused by quacks and fakers. The gift of agriculture has been misused to allow giant food surpluses on the one hand while hunger and starvation

62

go unrelieved on the other. The gift of creating wealth has been misused to produce inordinate riches on the one hand while abject poverty continues on the other. The gift of inventive genius has been misused to produce weapons to kill, gases to paralyze and bombs that can wipe out whole populations. The gift of communications has been misused to produce a nightmare of psychos, sex kittens, and occult horror on TV and theater screens. The gift of teaching has been misused to turn our public schools into an education in crime, narcotics and violence instead of the traditional three R's. The gift of law and order has been misused to build a network of corruption that reaches into city hall, the county courthouse and all the branches of our federal government. We are sinners both personally and socially.

Sin is separation from the Father. The young prodigal discovered the real meaning of life in the "far country." He had a lot of problems there. If we can believe his older brother, his problems were many. He gambled away the father's inheritance. He consorted with harlots. But these were not his real problem. His real problem was a wrong relationship with his father. When he severed his relationship with the father, he cut himself off from love and goodness. His basic need was a need for a restored relationship with the father. In the temptation in the wilderness, Jesus answered the Tempter's offers with the truth that it is more important to be right with the Father than it is to eat bread. A wrong relationship with God is always at the root of sinful living.

The prodigal did not fall into sin and then leave home. He left home, and then, separated from goodness and love, he went astray. This is true of us. When we choose to live without God, we cut ourselves off from His goodness and love. God is love. Hell is where God is not. Hell is lovelessness. Sinful living itself is God's judgment upon our sin. People try to deny the existence of God because it makes their sin easier to live with. Failing to deny Him, they defy Him and live in their sin. It is impossible to detach ethics and morality from faith. It is not accidental that the same decade that produced the "God is dead" theology also produced a new libertarian attitude toward sin that gave us sex without love and murder without guilt. People cannot live by bread alone or sex alone or money alone. People live, not because they ate bread yesterday, but because, in His grace, the Father wills that they live.

To be separated from God is a serious and perilous condition. If we forsake God's will, we fall into self-will. If we forsake the love of God, it is not difficult to despise and hate others. If we forsake the truth of God, we can easily believe in, and deal in, lies. Cutting ourselves off from God is as serious a hazard to spiritual life as doing without food is dangerous to the physical life. To become separated from God is to become deceived in the mind, hardened in the heart and weakened in the will. The end is spiritual death.

"Let no one say when he is tempted, 'I am being tempted by God'; for God cannot be tempted by evil, and He Himself does not tempt any one. But each one is tempted when he is carried away and enticed by his own lust. Then when lust has conceived, it gives birth to sin; and when sin is accomplished, it brings forth death" (James 1:13-15 NASB). Because sin has drawn us away from God, we need to go home to Him. When we come back to Him, we are "refathered." We are refathered in a new birth. But the parable in amazing grace lays the emphasis not on the loss of the son, but on the loss of the father. God loved the world and us so much that He is the one who feels the loss when we go astray. "The Lord is not slow about His promise, as some count slowness, but is patient toward you, not wishing for any to perish but for all to come to repentance" (II Peter 3:9 NASB). The incredible good news is that God cares so much that our sins really hurt Him more than they do us. Only that can explain the agony of Calvary.

Sin is giving up on God's purpose for our lives. David said, "You show me the path of life; in your presence there is fullness of joy, in your right hand are pleasures forevermore" (Psalms 16:11). What is your path of life? What is the purpose of your existence? Why are you here? God has a purpose for our lives and giving up on that purpose is sin. The new birth puts the purpose of God back in our lives. Our first question upon being restored to the Father's love is, "What do you want me to do?" People who leave God out of their lives become slaves to their attitudes, their appetites, their ambitions. People who discover God in Christ are set free to be all they can be and all they were meant to be. "For he who finds me finds life and obtains favor from the Lord, but he who forgets me injures himself; all who hate me love death" (Proverbs 8:35,36). The tragedy of human life upon this planet is an enigma shrouded in a mystery, without the purpose of God.

This is just as true about us personally as it is of our life together in society. What does God want us to do and be? In the new birth, God does not take over our lives. He does not wipe out our individuality and personality. He gives us our life goals. He gives us grace to reach those goals. The person in Christ has the "fruits of the Spirit." The nine fruits of the Spirit touch all the significant relationships of life. "But the fruit of the Spirit is love, joy, peace, patience, kindness, goodness, faithfulness, gentleness, self-control" (Galations 5:22 NASB). The first three relate to our relationship to God and give us a goal for the right kind of relationship with Him. To love God with all that we are and to enjoy Him forever, having His peace, is our first goal. This is the basic interpersonal relationship that must be right if we are to enjoy life in its fullness. It is God's purpose for us in relation to Himself. The next three virtues relate to other persons. To be patient, kind and good in all our relationships with our family, our friends, our fellow Christians, and all other persons, is our second goal.

All of these virtues are attitudinal and relational. We are just now discovering how important these interpersonal relationships are for those who are called upon to make critical decisions. The last three of the virtues are related to us as persons. To be faithful, gentle and self-controlled in our own personal lives is the third goal. If we want to be fit for ourselves to know, our lives will be characterized by faithfulness, gentleness and self-control.

Many people have difficulty liking other people because they really do not like themselves. These goals are as good and attainable for the laborer as they are for the lawyer, as good and attainable for the pipe fitter as they are for the physician, as good and attainable for the housewife as they are for the airline stewardess. The fruits of the Spirit are a direct consequence of the new birth. The nine virtues must be claimed by faith and cultivated with discipline in our lives. They are what David called "the Path of Life."

What Is Judgment?

Judgment, or punishment for sin, is almost always related in our minds to the future. People are inclined to believe that a timely or even "deathbed" repentance will allow them to escape judgment for sin. They are thinking of the human court of law which punishes sometime after the wrongdoing. In the story of the waiting father, the judgment comes with the offense. The consequences of sin are always immediate and inevitable. To say it another way, sin brings its own punishment. When a person chooses to live in distrust and disobedience to God, in suffering the immediate consequences of that distrust and disobedience, he is already under judgment. "He who believes in Him is not judged [present tense]; he who does not believe has been judged already [past tense], because he has not believed [past tense] in the name of the only begotten Son of God" (John 3:18). There is not one single future tense.

The truth of present judgment for sin is clearly taught in the epistle to the Romans. "The wrath of God is revealed [present tense] from heaven against all ungodliness and unrighteousness of men who trample underfoot the truth" (Romans 1:18). In the passage that follows, Paul three times says that "God gave them up" (Romans 1:24,26,28). God just turned them over to their own sin, and their own sin punished them.

A case in point is sexual sin. Paul says that homosexuality carries its own punishment. He says that "the depraved mind" will be punishment enough. All one needs to do is to observe the so-called "gay" people and one can see the judgment of God in operation. They are anything but gay. Frustration, guilt and self-recrimination bring their own punishment. The "depraved mind" has a built-in, immediate and inexorable judgment. Alcoholism brings its own punishment, in a diseased liver, disrupted family and the loss of self-respect. Sin is a radical disease and it takes a radical cure. The new birth is the only way that guilt can be erased and self-respect restored. It is not turning over a new leaf, it is a completely new life.

A recent letter to newspaper columnist Ann Landers appeared in one of her columns: "Dear Ann Landers: Yesterday was the saddest day of my life. I buried my mother. As I looked at her lovely kind face for the very last time, many thoughts crossed my mind. I recalled the times I meant to give her a phone call and ask if there was anything she needed. I seldom got around to it. I recalled the day I ran into Mom in the bakery. Her winter coat looked shabby and worn. I thought, 'Gee, I've got to take Mom downtown and buy her a coat.' But I was too busy. I recalled her last birthday. We sent an azalea plant but couldn't get over to see her. The East-West football game was on that afternoon and the boss was giving a party that night. I recalled the last time I saw Mom alive. It was at my cousin's wedding. She looked so old. I told myself, 'I must send Mom to Florida to visit her brother and get a little sun.' But I never got around to buying the ticket. If only I could turn the clock back, Ann. I'd buy Mom that coat, take her to the theater, spend every birthday with her, and send her any place she wanted to go. But it's too late."

See it clearly. This man has to live with that all of his life. That is punishment for sin. At the point of our mistreatment of others, there is always the possibility of finding God. We say, "I really treated her rough. It was really dirty. I'm a devil. What's wrong with me anyway?" Then we may see that the sin was really against God, because it hurt one of his creations. At that point, we may be on our way home again.

This emphasis on present and immediate judgment is not to deny that there is a future judgment. The future judgment centers on what we have done with God's offer of salvation in Jesus Christ. Sin has been judged in the cross of Jesus Christ and it has been judged in the life of the sinner. The future judgment is to affirm and confirm for eternity that choice we have made for Jesus Christ or that rejection of Jesus Christ. The description of the future judgment that Jesus left for us in Matthew 25 focuses on what we have done with Jesus Christ.

He has appeared to us in life in many ways. Our options were given to us. In chapter two of the epistle to the Romans, Paul says that, at the future judgment, "deeds" will be reviewed but man's final destiny is determined by what he has done with Jesus Christ (Romans 2:16). Future judgment, in the Book of Revelation, also focuses on what we have done and what we have done with Jesus Christ (Revelation 22:12,13). There is a day of judgment and retribution. All men have an appointment for that day. ". . . When the Lord Jesus shall be revealed from heaven with His mighty angels in flaming fire, dealing out retribution to those who do not know God and to those who do not obey the gospel of our Lord Jesus Christ. And these will pay the penalty of eternal destruction away from the presence of the Lord and from the glory of His power" (II Thessalonians 1:7-9).

Judgment is destitution. "Now when he had spent everything, a severe famine occurred in that country, and he began to be in need" (Luke 15:14 NASB). The poverty is not just material resources but life resources. The world around him is bankrupt and he has spent all of his own life's resources. The appetites and indulgence of those appetites yield ever decreasing pleasures. "By faith Moses, when he had grown up, refused to be called the son of Pharaoh's daughter; choosing rather to endure the ill treatment with the people of God, than to enjoy the passing pleasures of sin" (Hebrews 11:24,25 NASB). The longer you cultivate the soil of sin the less it yields. The alcoholic has less and less pleasure in his drinking that he cannot quit. The sensualist finds fewer and fewer nerve endings to titillate.

In contrast, love grows deeper and deeper. Joy in God increases in the pleasure it gives us. The pursuit of truth grows more and more exciting. Not only is the prodigal poor, but the world around him is helpless to give aid. A man can give himself to making money, but the more he makes the less pleasure he finds in it unless he is making that money for the good of others and the glory of God. God is saying to us that there is more, so much more to living than that filth for which we strive and lie and cheat and steal. At best, the pleasures of sin are only passing pleasures. The destitution may seem more real in regard to sensuality, but it is just as real in regard to attitudinal sin such as pride or a critical spirit. They destroy us just as viciously as alcoholism or drug addiction. Scrooge, in Dickens's Christmas masterpiece, is a good example of destitution surrounded by riches.

Judgment is degradation. For the prodigal son, a Jew, to become a swineherd in the employ of a Gentile was doubly degrading, according to Jewish thought at the time of Christ. There is nothing really wrong in being a shepherd to swine or any other animal, but the point was that a person can sink so low that he sees everything in terms of what he is slave to. Some people see everything in terms of cash. Others see everything in terms of the next "fix" or the next drink. Others may see everything in terms of obscenity. Even love and friendship can be degraded until they are seen in terms of what they can do for us. Recently, on a flight to New York, a young passenger was releasing a flood of obscenity and profanity. Everything he said was obscene. Finally, he could see that the passengers and the stewardess were quite sick of him. But he had no power to stop. He had degraded himself until he was no longer capable of carrying on a decent conversation. He had shame. He finally just became silent. He was not capable of maintaining communication without filth. He was obviously uncomfortable not having someone with whom to share his filth. Paul described such people: "And although they know the ordinance of God, that those who practice such things are worthy of death, they not only do the same, but also give hearty approval to those who practice them" (Romans 1:32 NASB).

Judgment is disappointment. The story of the prodigal son simply says that "no one was giving anything to him." The penalty of giving ourselves to something that is not worthy of us is inordinate desire. Drug pushers are not moved at all by the pitiful cries for another "fix" from their victims. Pimps are not moved at all by the shameful condition of the girls they have trapped. Persons have sold themselves for gain only to discover bitter disappointment in knowing that they bought "a pig in the poke." When our own plans have backfired and our lives are in ruins, the taste of disappointment is bitter in our mouth. Sometimes it is a position we worked and planned for that never comes. We give ourselves to the corporation and we wake up one day and we are forty-five and "over the hill" and it is too late. What we wanted so desperately we now know can never be ours. The disappointment can make us bitter and even critical of the person who passed us on the ladder of success. Then one day we get the word that the corporation will no longer be needing our services. Everything we believed in and worked for and planned for so well is gone.

What Is Repentance?

Disappointment, degradation and destitution can lead us to repentance. This is really the Father's purpose in so dealing with us. We feel that we are being destroyed. But the purpose of the judgment of God upon sin is not that the sinner may be destroyed, but that he might be saved. The prodigal takes three actions: "I will stand up" and "I will go" and "I will say." That is repentance.

It is willingness to turn around and go the other way. It is saying, "I've had enough of this filth that I am

71

lying in; I will stand up." That is it! Stand up, like a man, and look right into the face of God.

It is saying, "Why should I live as I am living? I will go home to the Father where there is bread and to spare!" It is saying, "I'm going to quit lying to myself. I am a sinner. I am to blame for the mess my life is in. I will say it again. I am a sinner."

Repentance is necessary for a new birth. The prodigal can never be "refathered" until he comes to this point. Pilate murdered some Galileans who may have been protesting Roman occupation. By accident, a falling tower killed some people looking on. This was reported to Jesus with the comment, "Those people must have been great sinners for a thing like that to happen to them?"

Jesus said, "I tell you no, but, unless you repent, you will all likewise perish" (Luke 13:3). Jesus was saying that all men are sinners, all men need to repent and, rather than going about trying to find out who the biggest sinners are, we had better take a good look at ourselves.

Repentance is reaching up for God out of our sin and misery. Shakespeare's Hamlet expresses the agony of not being able to repent when he says, "What can repentance? But what can it not? When one cannot repent? O bosom black as death." The one thing that the story of the waiting father cannot illustrate is that, in the case of God, He did not just wait for us to come home. He Himself, in Jesus Christ, came into the "far country." He came to the world in which we live to seek and to save us in our destitution, degradation and disappointment. Our Older Brother is not like the older brother of the story, who is actually annoyed because the younger son has returned and calls him "your son" and not "my brother."

Remember that Jesus Christ is the Son of God and we are the "sons of God." "But we do see Him who has been made for a little while lower than the angels, namely, Jesus, because of the suffering of death crowned with glory and honor, that by the grace of God He might taste death for every one. For it was fitting for Him, for whom are all things, and through whom are all things, in bringing many sons to glory, to perfect the author of their salvation through sufferings . . . for which reason He is not ashamed to call them brethren" (Hebrews 2:9-12 NASB).

When God's pardon for sin is offered, the question is raised, "Isn't God really treating my sin pretty lightly? All I have to do is get down and pray and it's all gone. Man, that's pretty easy." We are making two mistakes in saying this. First, God is not treating sin lightly. In making us suffer the consequences of sin, He has already judged sin in the sinner and in society. We do not break the law; the law breaks us. Secondly God only forgives sin on the basis of genuine repentance. Repentance literally means "a change of mind," but it has emotional content. It is deep sorrow over what we have done to God in sinning. It cannot be tears and a light promise to do better because we have been caught. An old piece of poetry makes light of repentance that is not real:

> *A Christian is a man who feels*
> *Repentance on a Sunday*
> *For what he did on Saturday*
> *And will do again on Monday.*

Real repentance is not a fear of the consequences of sin. It is sorrow that we have sinned against God to the point that our whole attitude is changed and we sincerely want God's help. It is seeing ourselves as God sees us. For the first time we really see ourselves as we are and we do not like what we see. The prodigal admitted it was not bad luck or his bad companions or his father's orders or his mother's nagging that got him into trouble, but his own sin. He knew who the real culprit was. What he saw filled him with disgust. "The hired servants of my father are better than I am," he thought.

73

One cannot say how intense the emotional reaction must be for repentance to be real, because all of us express our emotions differently. One thing is certain, that there is no real repentance if there is no feeling of pain because of what we have done toward God. The feeling leads to action. The action involves the will. Jesus appealed to the emotions and He appealed to the mind, but He appealed to them only to get at the will. The prodigal exercised the will when he said, "I will arise" and "I will go" and "I will say." The Latin word for repentance indicates a change of mind. The word "conversion" is related to the will. Conversion is the decision to change directions. It is turning to God. The new birth is the work of God and is God's part in changing man's nature. Conversion is related to man's side of the experience of new birth. Conversion is turning around and going in the other direction.

We were living our lives in self-will apart from God. "Touched by a loving heart and wakened by kindness," we see ourselves as sinners. When we turned away from our sin, that was repentance, and, when we turned toward God, that was faith. It is impossible to separate them. ". . . I did not shrink from declaring to you anything that was profitable, and teaching you publicly and from house to house, solemnly testifying to both Jews and Greeks of repentance toward God and faith in our Lord Jesus Christ" (Acts 20:20,21 NASB).

We must not forget the companion story of the lost sheep. It adds the one missing dimension of the Father's love. His love is a seeking love. God sent His Son on a mission of deliverance. He came and said, "I am the Good Shepherd." God actually seeks us in our sin. The very punishment that our own sin brings is Him seeking us. The woman looks eagerly for the lost coin and the Shepherd in concern looks for the lost sheep.

We must not forget that there is a clearer and

greater judgment on sin than that which the sinner suffers. It is that Word on the cross. That bloody man with five bleeding wounds bears all the sins of all the world. What he did bears upon our conscience a greater weight than all the judgment sin has brought us. What He did does more to bring us to repentance and faith in a new birth than anything else. That cross was not the end of Him in this world. He promised He would send the Helper, the Holy Spirit, to convince us of sin, of righteousness, and of judgment on sin.

Who made us remember with regret that we mistreated a loved one? Who helped us to think that we've got to stop drinking because it is getting to us? Who made us realize just last week that money isn't everything? Who made us feel guilty and dirty when we slept with another man's wife? It was the seeking God, the Shepherd of the one lost sheep coming to us. He is saying to us, "You must be born again." F.W. Faber has pictured it well for us:

> That was the Shepherd of the flock; He knew
>   The distant voice of one poor sheep astray;
> It had forsaken Him, but He was true,
>   And listen'd for its bleating night and day.
> Lost in a pitfall, yet alive it lay,
>   To breathe the faint sad call that He would know;
> But now the slighted fold was far away,
>   And no approaching footsteps soothed its woe. . . .
>
> And so He came and raised it from the clay,
>   While evil beasts went disappointed by.
> He bore it home along the fearful way
>   In the soft light of His rejoicing eye.
> And thou fallen soul afraid to live or die
>   In the deep pit that will not set thee free,
> Lift up to Him the helpless homeward cry,
>   For all that tender love is seeking thee.

What can I believe? Everything I have learned about God and the life to come, I am no longer sure about all that. Barrington's class in anthropology has made me question everything I ever believed. Am I the "naked ape" or the creation of God? I'm so mixed up. I used to be so sure of everything. What would Mom and Dad think if they knew I was having all these doubts? Elmore's class in mathematics is just the opposite. He believes everything about God. Which one of them is right? How am I to know which one to believe?

If Barrington is right, then what's the use of all this church business and trying to live right. I want to have some fun, to do some of the things I never even wanted to do when I was at home. I've got to get rid of those old-fashioned ideas about God and sex. That's what Marge said. She is some kind of girl. She really turns me on. I can just imagine what Mom would say if she met her. If I ever marry a girl, she'll be like Mom, but Marge is fun.

My problem is that I'm damned if I do and I'm damned if I don't. When I'm with Marge and her crowd I really like it. Then I go to Elmore's class and he talks about God like he really knows Him. I get all shook up. My parents always seemed to be so sure—the preacher at home, too. When I think of how I used to believe everything they told me. I never really doubted anything they said until now. I wonder, do I really need to believe?

76

4.

THE NEED TO BELIEVE

"Now He was telling them a parable to show that at all times they ought to pray and not lose heart, saying, 'There was in a certain city a judge who did not fear God, and did not respect man. And there was a widow in that city, and she kept coming to him, saying, "Give me legal protection from my opponent." And for a while he was unwilling; but afterward he said to himself, "Even though I do not fear God nor respect man, yet because this widow bothers me, I will give her legal protection, lest by continually coming she wear me out."'

"And the Lord said, 'Hear what the unrighteous judge said; now shall not God bring about justice for His elect, who cry to Him day and night, and will He delay long over them? I tell you that He will bring about justice for them speedily. However, when the Son of Man comes will He find faith on the earth?'" (Luke 18:1-18 NASB).

In *Today's English Version* of the Bible, Luke says that Jesus told this parable that "they should always pray and never become discouraged." Did you ever get discouraged and quit praying? Do you recall that black day when God appeared to you to be "an unjust judge?" Perhaps on that day you laid into a little grave the sunshine of your life? Or was it on that day when the one who promised to love and cherish you "until death do us part" told you that he or she just didn't care anymore? Or was it that day when your wife called you at work and told you that your daughter had run away? Or it may have been that day when the doctor told you, "I am sorry, Bill, but you have cancer." Or was it that day when the boss told you that the company no longer needed your services and you were fifty-nine and very frightened? Or was it that day when you sat on the edge of your wife's hospital bed and the doctor said, "I am sorry to have to tell you but your new son is seriously deformed and will probably be retarded?" Or that day when you discovered that a business partner had ruined you, and the business you worked so hard to build was gone? Are you like Dinny, in John Galsworthy's *Maid in Waiting,* who says to her mother when they are discussing religion, "I suppose there is an eternal plan for us but we are like all the gnats for all the care it has of us."

Dinny cannot even refer to God as "he" or "God" but uses the neuter pronoun, "it." Is God so impersonal and so unmoved by your predicament that He does not appear to you as "God" but "it"? Or, like the helpless widow in our parable, does He appear to you to be "an unjust judge" because life has treated you so unfairly? For many years this parable was a mystery to me. How could Jesus say that God was like "an unjust judge?" What is even worse one almost has to see in the word, "unrighteous," the fact that this judge was crooked. He probably was "on the take." Then one day, when I was reading it, like a spiritual sunrise, the light came, and I saw what Jesus was trying to say to us. The key is in verses seven and eight. Jesus says, "God is not like the crooked judge who delays and delays, perhaps trying to get a bribe.

He answers speedily." You see, Jesus was trying to get us to see that God appears to us to be an unjust judge in our sin and unbelief. There are many people who become very upset and very angry when one even begins to talk about God to them. They are not really angry with us. They are angry at God because they believe that He has treated them unfairly.

Years after I had been the pastor of a small church, I returned to that church for special services. They had just completed a beautiful building in the midst of a small rural community and they were very proud of it. One afternoon, the pastor suggested that we visit a man who was not a Christian. I did not share with the pastor that, as a young pastor, I had known this man, whose name was John. I had fished and hunted with his son until the boy was tragically killed in a farm accident. I had the funeral for the boy and I remembered how hard and bitter John became. Years had gone by, however, and years sometimes have a way of softening hearts, so I looked forward to the visit. When we got out of the car at the farm, John was working on some machinery in the barn lot. The pastor led the way and, when we came to the gate that led into the barn lot, John stopped working and yelled, "I want you damn preachers to get off my property right now." The pastor tried to calm him but he reached down and picked up a crowbar he had been using and lifted it up and started toward the pastor. I said, "Fred, leave and let me see if I can talk to him," and Fred returned to the car.

I started, "Mr. Conway, do you remember me? I'm John Havlik. You remember that Joe and I hunted and fished together? I was the pastor of the church and I preached at Joe's funeral."

He hesitated, appearing for a moment to soften, and then his face hardened and he raised the crowbar and answered, "I mean you, too. Get off my land. What

79

you said at the funeral were lies. God took my boy and I'll never go near that church again."

On the way back to the church, I told Fred the story. He had been the pastor for only a short time and did not know it. I said, "Fred, John is not mad at us. He is mad at God. He believes that God killed his son. He believes that God is 'the unjust judge.'"

I would have given anything and everything if John had just given me time to make him face the truth about Joe. Joe was killed when a tractor seat collapsed and caused him to fall back into a "bush hog," a very large rotary mower designed to cut down brush. I knew, too, that John was in a hurry to get on with his work and had rigged up that seat with some wire. John was a "workaholic," but he did not take the time to weld the seat on the old tractor securely. He had killed Joe. He could never face it.

It is so easy to blame God or "fate" or "luck" for our blunders. This is our need to believe. If John could have come to God and confessed openly and honestly, "God, I killed Joe. I was in such a hurry. I didn't fix that seat right. God, I did it and I am sorry. Help me, God, and forgive me," in that moment, He would have been "refathered." In the new birth, he would have discovered a God who really cares. In experiencing the forgiveness of the heavenly Father, he would have been able to forgive himself. He would have been delivered of that load of guilt. In that moment when his face softened, he may have been close to the Kingdom of God. In the next moment, when his face hardened, he was light-years away.

Those who hear about the new birth experiences of people who were in trouble and then came to God may say, "The new birth is for 'losers.' Life success," they say, "is just having true grit, and people who do not have true grit find an escape from failure in a religious experience." What they really cannot see is that we are

80

all losers without God. The word from Isaiah, the prophet, is so lovely that it is poetry:

> *All of us like sheep have gone astray,*
> *Each of us has turned to his own way;*
> *But the Lord has caused the iniquity of us all*
> *To fall on Him.*

I can hear a reader asking, "Now that is right about John. He was really to blame. But what about the flood that came and swept away everything I owned? What about that? Are you going to blame that on me too?"

At least, I do not want you, dear reader, to blame God. I can remember the flood on the Ohio River. We cut all the trees off the hills to make barrels for Louisville whiskey. We filled the river bed with junk automobiles. We polluted the river with sewage from Cincinnati, Louisville, and every other city along the river. We paved thousands of acres that could not then soak up rain. The flood came and we blamed God. Did we blame Him because we did not want to "pay the piper"?

I even hear some people say, after an automobile accident, "I wonder why God took my boy?" If a drunk driver was involved, God didn't do it. If a violation of rules of traffic was involved, God didn't do it. If excessive speed was involved, God didn't do it.

Another says, "What about the weather?" Insurance companies may like to call weather-related accidents "acts of God," but, in most cases, one can discover the foolishness of man. Do you stay out on the golf course during thunderstorms? If you do, you must not blame God if you are struck by lightning.

What does all of this have to do with being born again? It has everything to do with it, because it is only in this sense of loss, of guilt, of frustration and of desperation that we turn to God. We turn to Him even though, like the helpless widow of our parable, we believe Him to be an unust judge.

We could learn a lot about God from our own families. How many of us have had or know someone who has had a teenager who believed his father to be an authoritarian unfair tyrant who was always making demands on him but never really loved him? Then some experience caused him to see his father through new eyes. Perhaps he ran away from home. He was picked up by the police in a strange city with some companions he met along the way. He did not know that they had hard drugs in the car. Reluctantly, he tells the police his name and address. His parents are called. The next morning, after a night in a jail cell, he is taken to a room. The officer opens a door and says, "Your father is in there."

The boy enters slowly and sees his father sitting at a table with his face buried in his hands, sobbing. Now he sees his father through new eyes. "He really cares," the boy is thinking. "He really cares." The boys says, "Dad . . ."

The father looks up, gets up, and runs to his son, taking him in his arms. The boy hears him saying, "Son, I love you. It will be all right. I will take care of it. Only, never do this again. Son, I love you so much. I couldn't stand it if you did it again."

Now he knows that his father cares. He knows his father loves. He knows that his sin has hurt the father. Down deep in his heart, he is saying, "I'll never do it again." He is "refathered." He never really knew what his father was like. It is like being born again. The word from Isaiah really came alive for that boy on that day. "But the Lord has caused the iniquity of us all to fall on Him."

Why did Jesus make so much of prayer in the parable? Prayer is asking God for something. "And I say to you, ask, and it shall be given to you. . . . For everyone who asks, receives . . ." (Luke 11:9,10 NASB). Our faith in God is not based upon our daily assent to a creed or a doctrine, but on daily prayer. The need to pray is a confession of our need for God and a confession that He is real in our lives. We may even accept with our minds the fact of God and yet really not believe. Belief is a result of the need to believe.

In that same rural church where I came to know John, I discovered this truth about prayer. One woman, May, was like a mother to me. I was very young and her son, Bill, was about my age. In my youth, I thought all Christians could lead in public prayer. One Sunday, in the evening service, I asked May to lead the congregation in prayer. She tried to pray and then broke down and cried. After the service she said, "Brother John, I just cannot pray in public. If you ever call on me again, I will embarrass you and you will embarrass me."

Several months later, in a hospital corridor just outside a room where her son Bill lay dying on his eighteenth birthday, she got down on her knees and asked me to kneel beside her while she prayed aloud. She was not embarrassed. She was eloquent in pouring out her heart to God. She paid no attention to curious visitors who passed by us. Her fears were gone. She had suddenly become the helpless widow of the parable. There was a frighteningly fearful need to believe.

Our praying for the most part is really not praying at all. We are so quick to say, "Your will be done." The pious people who say this so easily are really not praying at all. God has given us the right and privilege to speak to Him about everything which concerns us. But our quick slick prayers really never reach God. Salvation in a new birth which makes the Father real to us can never come from praying like that.

An eighteen-year-old girl, who has run away from home, gets off the bus in Atlanta. She has never gone to church or Sunday school. In the bus station a well-dressed but flashy man sees her and asks her if she is looking for work. She, in her innocence, cannot recognize a pimp. She finds herself in a cheap hotel room being raped and cries out, "O God, if there is a God, help me." Her prayer will come much closer to getting through to God in spite of her irreligion than a lot of the slick Sunday morning prayers that repeat meaningless phrases and religious jargon that surely must bore the Almighty.

The God of the Bible, the Jesus of the New Testament, is the One we can trust. There are no limits to His goodness or His power. But to believe only that is not a real basis for faith. "You believe that God is one. You do well; the demons also believe, and shudder" (James 2:19 NASB). Jesus says that we do well to believe in God, but that is not saving faith. No matter how great and good God is, we cannot trust Him unless there is an agreement between us. Faith in another person implies a trust relationship with that person. People came to Jesus with definite needs. Some needed sight, others needed food, and others needed mental health. They trusted Him and He met their need.

Many persons who are members of the church believe what the demons believe and in that "they do well." It is not enough to know that He is a healer; we must know that He has healed us. It is not enough to know that He is a great Savior; we must know that He has saved us. It is not enough to know that He can forgive sin; we must know that He has forgiven us.

The new birth is an experience with God in Jesus Christ in which He has met our need. We can know that He created the world without letting this knowledge affect us one way or another. We must know that He has "created us to good works" (Ephesians 2:10). This is what experiential faith is all about. The one definition of saving faith in the New Testament is a clear explanation of the kind of faith that finds God experientially. "And without faith it is impossible to please Him, for He who comes to God must believe that He is, and that He is a rewarder of those who seek Him" (Hebrews 11:6 NASB).

"To believe that He is" is not the crux of saving faith. It is to believe "that He is the rewarder of those who seek Him." In short, do we believe that God will do what He has said he would do? If I meet Him with my need, will He give me new life, new hope and a new name? We have the testimony of His word, and we have the testimony of many who have had an experience with Him which they call the new birth. Will He do for me what He has done for others? This is the contract that I have with Him. I brought Him my need with all the faith that I have. He met my need. He has not solved all my problems for me. He has not tricked me. He has done just what He said He would do.

He is the Man for others. He is the One who meets human need. If Jesus Christ came to Atlanta some beautiful Sunday morning at 10:15 a.m., where would we find him? I think we have a clue in the New Testament: In the synagogue at Nazareth, He stood before the people and opened the sacred scrolls to Isaiah the prophet and read, "The Spirit of the Lord is upon Me, because He anointed Me to preach the gospel to the poor. He has sent Me to proclaim release to the captives, and recovery of sight to the blind, to set free those who are downtrodden, to proclaim the favorable year of the Lord" (Luke 4:18,19 NASB).

Would He visit a Southern Baptist church because they are the largest group of evangelicals in America? Would He visit a Roman Catholic church because they have apostolic succession? Would He be in the church with the best building or the best music?

I think not. If we wanted to see Him, we would probably have to go down to some poor home where we would find Him with dirty, undernourished children on His knee. He would be telling them about the

Father's house. James Russell Lowell expresses it very well in "His Throne Is with the Outcast":

I followed where they led,
  And in a hovel rude,
With naught to fence the weather from his head,
  The King I sought for meekly stood;
A naked hungry child
  Clung round his gracious knee,
And a poor hungry slave looked up and smiled
  To bless the smile that set him free;
New miracles I saw his presence do,
  No more I knew the hovel bare and poor,
The gathered chips into a woodpile grew
  The broken morsel swelled to goodly store.
I knelt and wept: my Christ no more I seek.
  His throne is with the outcast and the weak.

"When the Son of Man comes, will He find faith on the earth?" The whole matter of prayer and faith that saves are related to the return of Jesus Christ. In all the great prayer passages of the New Testament, there are references to the second coming of Jesus Christ. The widow of our parable (Luke 18:1-9) was not just concerned about the return of her property but the matter of her existence. Her future was involved in her pleading. Our Lord was intensely practical and dealt very much in detail with our lives here and now. He was very much concerned with our interpersonal relationships in this life. He is saying in regard to the present that our great concern is not that there is a God "up there" who is listening, but whether there is anyone "down here" who is praying, who has faith in God.

This question relates the new birth to eternal life. The whole matter of destiny, future life, coming judgment, heaven and hell are at stake in our choice of or rejection of Jesus Christ. Jesus is reminding us of this in the parable. He is saying to us, "The woman pleads so earnestly, so unceasingly, because her whole future is at stake. I am concerned that you do not become discouraged and stop praying. I want you to know that it is not just a matter of your making a right decision now. There is at stake the whole matter of eternity, the future. The most important question in regard to eternity is not the question of whether or not there is a God who listens. The most important thing for you is, do you have life right now that settles the future?"

Your present faith is the guarantee that there will always be someone praying, someone with faith, someone who knows that He is not an "unjust judge" but the loving, caring Father. For us it means not only life now, but eternal life.

"I Don't Need to Believe"

Jean-Paul Sartre is in many ways the father of those who say today that they do not need belief, that faith is a relic of the past that needs to be put in the attic along with butter churns and bustles. In his *Age of Reason,* he gives us the testimony of those who have discarded both traditional faith and conventional morality. It is not a sin, but an obligation to question both traditional faith and conventional morality. It was a search for truth that led men to question the traditional belief that the world was flat because the Bible mentioned "the four corners of the earth." It was a search for truth that led youth in the 1960s to question the conventional morality that approved the Vietnam war.

Jesus was the greatest warrior who has ever lived against what was false in conventional morality and traditional faith. What is wrong with Sartre and his disciples is that they feel that no faith in the supernatural is possible for the man of intelligence and that there is no morality except what seems right at the moment. We have pointed out that what we have at the moment is not a generation of no faith. We have, instead, a superstitious generation who believe in gods that are not gods.

Man has to believe in something. Millions who gamble believe in "lady luck." We have a rash of gurus and syncretistic religions that serve up a hash of Christianity and mysticism. Both the "Moonies" and Campus Crusade have been accused of mixing religion with right-wing politics. And astrology and occult Oriental and Eastern religions have the loyalty of millions of our citizens.

Is it any wonder that, with all this, the "thinking man" says, "I don't need to believe." In the church, there are millions who call themselves religious without believing in God. They claim to be Christians but do not accept and live in the light of what is central to the Christian faith. Sartre, who recommends faith in nothing, really gives us faith in everything. One cannot say that man grows up and no longer needs a faith. There is that "God-shaped blank" in every human life that is constantly demanding to be filled. It is quite a commentary that an unbeliever should write that "man is incurably religious."

Jesus said, "Man cannot live by bread only," to the Tempter in the wilderness. Huxley, in his *Reason without Revelation,* argued that man can be religious without accepting any of the supernatural events of the gospel. It was people like that who gave us gas ovens for Jews. Man sweeps out old beliefs and cleans his house well only to discover that, for the one demon he has swept out, seven have returned (Matthew 12:43-45).

"I do not need to believe, because belief has nothing to do with behavior." It is strange that the age of Victoria should produce the fathers of this idea. Both

88

Thomas Huxley and John Morley were circumspect in their behavior. But how much of their "good behavior" was rooted in the culture that was so influenced by the Bible and faith in the supernatural? Do these people produce disciples who are as zealous for good works as their teachers? Can we depend on this kind of morality to sustain resources for building the future?

One of the reasons for this thinking was that the church, in the Victorian age, continued to separate its faith from the problems of slavery, the exploitation of colonial peoples, and the abominable working conditions of the average man. Because faith seemed unrelated to morality, it was argued that we do not need faith in order to behave. Today many of the leaders of industry, banking and production who are nominal Christians give little evidence of relating their faith to ecology, the problems of poverty and poor housing. Thinking young people say, "What need is there for me to believe?" It would help us to remember that there is a world of difference in intellectual assent to the Christian faith and an experiential faith in Jesus Christ as Lord whereby His life is lived in us. The person whose faith is nothing more than intellectual can no more be expected to practice Christian morality than a primitive tribe in the rain forest of the upper Amazon can be expected to practice WASP (White Anglo-Saxon Protestant) morality. Elizabeth Barrett Browning has expressed this failure of "good men" whose goodness is divorced from faith:

> *Good critics who have stamped out poets' hope,*
> *Good statesmen who pulled ruin on the state,*
> *Good patriots who for a theory risked a cause,*
> *Good kings who disemboweled for a tax,*
> *Good popes who brought all good to jeopardy,*
> *Good Christians who sat still in easy chairs*
> *And damned the general world for standing up—*
> *Now may the good God pardon all good men.*

"I do not need to believe because, for a Christian, believing is agreeing to an abstract, fuzzy and non-communicative theology."

A Harvard student, on vacation after his first year there, was telling me about his experience at the university. I asked, "Did you have an opportunity to hear and meet some interesting and dynamic Christians?"

He said, "All the Christians I heard were squares," drawing in the air a figure of a square with his finger. "The only dynamic people I heard or met were communists or hippies."

This is unfortunate when there are millions of people who have been changed by Jesus Christ in a new birth. They have the dynamism and enthusiasm of an experiential faith in Jesus Christ. There is a need for a logical system of faith in the Christian community but it has no place on the streets. It is more important to know that Jesus Christ has changed our lives than it is to know the theories as to the nature of the atonement. "Christ died for me" is the only theology of the atonement a witnessing Christian needs. What we are saying is that the simple (but not simplistic) faith of the born again Christian is easy to understand. The following is a simple experience or theology that we can share with others when we have had an experience of new birth: "Jesus Christ is the Son of God who offers me eternal life if I will repent of my sins and turn to Him and follow Him. In this experience of repenting and believing, we are changed by Jesus Christ. This change is so sudden, dramatic and revolutionary that it is like being born all over again. We call it the new birth, as Jesus did. We do not understand all the mysteries of how He gives us eternal life. We just know He did, because it was a personal experience with Him. We are not perfect, but He lives in us. He gives us His Holy Spirit to lead and guide us. After He comes into our lives, we are never the same. We know He wants us to live as He lived, love as He loved, die to selfish desires as He died for us." Really, this is all the theology that matters.

While a student in the university (not a Christian university) I had a professor of philosophy who was not a Christian. Because we were both Bohemians (real ones, whose ancestors came from one of the oldest kingdoms in eastern Europe), we were attracted to one another. He knew I was a Christian, but he did not know I was preparing for the professional Christian ministry at the time. He was made in the likeness of Huxley and Morley. He rejected everything supernatural, but was an evangelist for a strict puritanical moral code. After class one day he and I talked about something he had said that I could not accept because of my faith. He said, "John, you are an intelligent young man; how can you accept the ridiculous miracle stories of the Bible?"

I answered, "Professor, I cannot argue with you about religion or philosophy or the Bible, because you know much more about all of them than I do. But will you let me tell you about what happened to me?" He gave me permission to share my faith. I told him how, when I was eighteen years old, Jesus Christ had taken the hatred in my heart that I had for someone, and put love in its place. I related to him how God had changed me, my family and my friends in Jesus Christ.

When I had finished sharing my simple theology of the new birth, he said, "John, I cannot argue with that."

No one can. It happened to me, and I am an authority, not on theology or philosophy, but on what has happened to me. This I believe.

The Need for Meaning

I need to believe because, without belief in the supernatural, life really has no meaning. Even those who have given up on the supernatural have sought to find some meaning in the existence of man upon this planet. Murray has it right in Herb Gardner's play, *A Thousand Clowns,* when he says to the social worker who has come to take Norman, his nephew, away from him, "I want him to stay with me. . . . I want him to know exactly the special thing that he is. . . . And I want him to know the subtle sneaky important reason why he was born a human being and not a chair." How can my life have meaning with no relation to the eternal? The wise man, in the book of Ecclesiastes in the Old Testament, after relating the despair of ancient man as he looked at a silent sky and the futility of human life says, "But He has set eternity in our hearts."

Modern man suffers, as men have always suffered, from an identity crisis. We need to know "that subtle sneaky important reason why we were born a human being and not a chair." There are no easy answers, but Jesus Christ offers us answers that satisfy both our reaching out horizontally to our fellows and vertically to God. He says that the summation of the whole law is loving God with all of our capacities and loving our neighbors as ourselves.

The best illustration of the search for meaning can be found in the counter-culture of the 1960s. This culture was in revolt against the meaninglessness of the society in which we lived. These young people, some of whom called themselves "hippies," experimented with many things in trying to find meaning. They rediscovered the Christian doctrine of man and shook up the church, great corporations and our educational system with their searchings. They knew that man was more important than institutions, the almighty dollar and the American success ethic. They experimented with drugs, unrestrained sex, and the monastic life in their searching. Then in the late 1960s and early 1970s they rediscovered the Christian doctrine of

God. They claimed a new birth. There was excess in some groups, but many of these societies of reborn young Christians pointed the way back to renewal and revival for the denominational churches. They had opted for Jesus Christ.

Like Saul of Tarsus, many young militants found the Prince of Peace. Society claims that it desires to rehabilitate the criminal. But then, when a reborn Eldridge Cleaver returns to society, reclaimed by Jesus Christ, that same society calls his religion a "cop out." Eldridge found the meaning of life and he found it in a born again experience with Jesus Christ.

The Need for Forgiveness

If our first problem is meaninglessness, our second is guilt. All the literature of all civilizations attests to man's deep sense of guilt. How many bouquets of flowers are given to a wife because of guilt over some assignation? How many tears shed over a coffin are not for grief but for guilt? How many new toys and even vitamin pills are given children, not out of concern for their welfare, but because of guilt over a whipping that was too violent or neglect that left even greater scars.

Once, a girl who looked young enough to be playing with dolls came to me after a service and asked to talk with me. She had two small children with her. She said, "I just don't understand me. I ran away from home and married a guy who got me pregnant and then left me. I broke my daddy's heart. He died with a heart attack three months after I left. I hurt my mother who is still living. I am married again and this man is really good to me. He works hard. He doesn't drink or nothin'. But I get mad at him and curse him. I whip the children. I am afraid sometime I will really hurt them when I am so mad. What's wrong with me?"

I had to tell her, "Darling, you are living in a hell on earth. It is your hell. You made it. You have never forgiven yourself for what you did to your parents. I think the reason you have never forgiven yourself is that you are not certain that God has forgiven you." After more conversation, I had the joy of leading her into experiencing the forgiving love of God and the "peace that exceeds our ability to understand" (Philippians 4:7).

I have always enjoyed looking at old tombstones. Some of them have poetry on them. Some even have humor. One very old tombstone I have seen has only one word carved on it, "FORGIVEN." There was no name, no date of birth or death, just the one great word, *forgiven*. All kinds of thoughts ran through my mind. How many stories one can imagine! A prodigal comes home and dies in his daddy's arms. A wayward daughter is found and dies of some dread disease contracted in her terrible life. A husband who was unfaithful to his vows of marriage and violated the marriage trust in the bed of another man's wife. Who wrote those words? A loving father? A faithful mother? A true and good wife? No one knows. But it is a beautiful word——forgiven.

In my ministry as a pastor, I have seen people forgive one another. People are most beautiful when they forgive. People are most like God when they forgive. The greatest words ever spoken may have been those words from the Hill of the Skull when He cried out, "Father, forgive them. They don't know what they are doing" (Luke 23:24). He freely forgave those cruel hands that bared forever the heart that loves those who hate Him. There is no greater love. We need forgiveness.

94

The Need for Courage

Paul Tillich and others have said that man's basic needs are at the points of meaning, guilt and fear of dying. The more civilized man becomes and the farther away from nature and nature's God he gets, the more feverishly he works at taking away the sting of death. The one thing that man does not want to face is death. He spends more money on dying than he does on all the mission work and charitable work now going on in the world. The most unchristian thing about the average Christian's death is the funeral. It only reinforces the fact that we are so afraid of death that we try to hide it.

The Christian has an obligation to tell the truth about death, not to hide its horror. The hands we touched and held, the lips we kissed, the eyes into which we looked and saw love are rotting in the grave. This is the truth. If that body is all there is then it is all over for them and will soon be all over for us. The person who does not believe in the supernatural must believe what a poet of unbelief wrote concerning death:

> From too much love of living,
>   From hope and fear set free,
> We thank with brief thanksgiving
>   Whatever gods may be
> That no life lives forever;
> That dead men rise up never;
>   That even the weariest river
>   Winds somewhere safe to sea.

But there is more. There is a resurrection. That body that rots in the grave is no more the person than a

95

house is a family. In Christ, the whole personality lives through a new birth. The person shall have a new body, a spiritual body of resurrection. How different from the lines of the poet of unbelief are these lines from Horatio Bonar:

> *I change, He changes not,*
> *The Christ can never die;*
> *His love, not mine, the resting place,*
> *His truth, not mine, the tie.*
> *The cross still stands unchanged,*
> *Though heaven is now His home;*
> *The mighty stone is rolled away,*
> *But yonder is His tomb.*
>
> *And yonder is my peace,*
> *The grave of all my woes;*
> *I know the Son of God has come,*
> *I know He died and rose.*
> *I know He liveth now*
> *At God's right hand above;*
> *I know the throne on which He sits,*
> *I know His truth and love.*

"Now if Christ is preached, that He has been raised from the dead, how do some among you say that there is no resurrection from the dead? But if there is no resurrection of the dead, not even Christ has been raised. . . . But now, Christ has been raised from the dead, the first fruits of those who are asleep" (I Corinthians 15:12,13,20 NASB). Only Christ can light a candle of hope in the darkness and horror of the grave. Sin has met its conqueror in Jesus Christ. He has broken the law of sin and death in the law of the spirit and life (Romans 8:2). In the new birth, one is born of God and the "seed of God remains in him." "No one who is born of God keeps on practicing sin, because His seed remains in him; and he cannot keep

96

on practicing sin, because he is born of God" (I John 3:9). "Some will say, 'How are the dead raised? With what kind of body will they come out of death?' . . . God gives it a body just as He wishes, and to each of the seeds a body of its own. . . . So is the resurrection of the body" (I Corinthians 15:35,38,42). Paul is saying that the seed by which we were born again guarantees a new body, a spiritual body. Those who do not have that hope in them are of all men most miserable. We need courage for living and for dying.

The Need for Salvation

Perhaps all of our needs may be stated in one word, salvation. This is a great word which describes how God delivers me from the power, practice and presence of sin. It is God's work in my life from my new birth to the gift of my glorified body in resurrection. All of us know that we are sinners, but only a few know the consequences of our sins.

Paul says that the law is our schoolmaster, to bring us to salvation in Christ. The law shows us that we are sinners; That, however little the light we have, we never live up to that light. In the new birth, God saves us from the guilt and power of sin. In my daily experiences, as I grow as a Christian into Christlikeness, I am being saved from the practice of sin. When I shall see Him "face to face" in my glorified body to live with Him eternally, I will be saved from the presence of sin. All of this is salvation.

The salvation experience, including our earthly pilgrimage and our heavenly experience, begins with the new birth. Without birth, there is no life, and, without life, there is no resurrection of life. When we call upon God for salvation, we are asking Him for an experience that stretches from this moment through eternity.

The hardest words to say are the words, "I have sinned." We do have a way of blaming others. The game of "passing the buck" began in Eden when Adam replied to the Lord, "The woman you gave me, gave the fruit to me, and I did eat." Isn't this the game we all play day after day? Rebellious youths blame their parents. Young rebels blame society. The alcoholic blames his wife. It is all because we cannot face up to the fact that we are sinners.

The Scriptures say that we are sinners (I Kings 8:46; Ecclesiastes 7:20; Isaiah 53:6; Romans 3:23, Galatians 3:20; I John 1:8). Experience says we are sinners. Ask anyone about yourself. Ask them if they think you are perfect. What will their answer be? The theater, the arts, literature, all say we are sinners. The plot of almost every story, every play, every TV show is man's sin. It is not easy for us to see that sin is against God. We can *wrong* other people, but we *sin* against God. Something that wrongs a person, made in God's image, is also a sin against God. David sees it correctly when, having wronged a man, a woman and his people, he says, "Against thee, thee only, have I sinned" (Psalms 51:4 AV).

The best word for sin is that word given to us by John in his first epistle, "Every one who practices sin also practices lawlessness; and sin is lawlessness" (I John 3:4 NASB). Obedience is the law regarding our relationship to God. Holiness is the law in relationship to ourselves. Love is the law in relationship to others. "If we say that we have no sin, we are deceiving ourselves, and the truth is not in us" (I John 1:8 NASB). We cannot hide our sin. We cannot explain away our sin. Because we are sinners by nature, by practice and by association, we need a Savior. Nothing less than a new birth can deliver us from the bondage of sin. Christ wants to set us free (redeem us) from

98

our bondage to sin. God has dealt with sin in a radical and serious way. His estimate of the seriousness of sin is seen in the tragedy of the cross. He offers us salvation from sin and its power, beginning with a new birth.

You need to believe. For your meaninglessness, there is His meaning. For your guilt, there is His forgiveness. For your fear, there is His courage. For your sin, there is His salvation. You are the helpless widow. You are the praying one. Lift your eyes and heart to God and, with all the faith you have, ask Him to come into your life. Ask Him to forgive your sin. If you are not yet convinced that He is as loving and forgiving as I have said, go to Him anyway. You will find that He is not an unjust judge. There is a hymn of invitation, written by George C. Stebbins, that we sing. It expresses very well how we must come to Him:

> Out of my bondage, sorrow, and night,
>   Jesus, I come, Jesus, I come;
> Into thy freedom, gladness, and light,
>   Jesus, I come to thee;
> Out of my sickness into thy health,
> Out of my want and into thy wealth,
> Out of my sin and into thyself,
>   Jesus, I come to thee.
>
> Out of the fear and dread of the tomb,
>   Jesus, I come, Jesus, I come;
> Into the joy and light of thy home,
>   Jesus, I come to thee;
> Out of the depths of ruin untold,
> Into the peace of thy sheltering fold,
> Every thy glorious face to behold,
>   Jesus, I come to thee.

I believe in God. I have always believed. Why does she keep talking to me about a "new birth"? I am not some kind of heathen. I'm as good as the next guy. I know I can't talk to God like she does—she's always talking to Him. I love her. I want to marry her. She keeps telling me that she wants me to be a "real Christian" first. I'm a Christian. I always have been one. I think there is a God up there somewhere. You don't know Him like you do another person. You're not always talking to Him like Mary Ellen does. I wish she would quit bugging me about it.

She says that, when you really know Him, He is "your personal Savior." I never heard of that in the church I grew up in. Maybe if I started going to my church again she would be happy. I'd really like to know God the way she does. He sounds "for real" when she talks about Him. Does God really take the time to talk to her or to me? It always seemed to me He was way up above everything, that He really didn't know or didn't care what's going on down here.

She talks about God and you almost believe that God has nothing to do except take care of her. She keeps saying, "My Father this" and "My Father that." I've always thought of Him as "the" God but never "my" God. I don't know if I can take that all my life, but I love her. I'll either have to give her up or find out more about God than I know now. Can He be "my God," just as if I was the only person in the whole world?

100

5.

THIS IS MY GOD

"When therefore it was evening on that day, the first day of the week, and when the doors were shut where the disciples were, for fear of the Jews, Jesus came and stood in their midst and said to them, 'Peace be with you.' And when He had said this, He showed them both His hands and His side. The disciples therefore rejoiced when they saw the Lord.

"Jesus therefore said to them again, 'Peace be with you; as the Father has sent Me, I also send you.' And when He had said this, He breathed on them, and said to them, 'Receive the Holy Spirit. If you forgive the sins of any, their sins have been forgiven them; if you retain the sins of any, they have been retained.'

"But Thomas, one of the twelve, called Didymus, was not with them when Jesus came. The other disciples therefore were saying to him, 'We have seen the Lord!'

"But he said to them, 'Unless I shall see in His hands the imprint of the nails, and put my finger into the place of the nails, and put my hand into His side, I will not believe.' And after eight days again His disciples were inside, and Thomas with them.

Jesus came, the doors having been shut, and stood in their midst, and said, 'Peace be with you.' Then He said to Thomas, 'Reach here your finger, and see My hands; and reach here your hand, and put it into My side; and be not unbelieving, but believing.'

"Thomas answered and said to Him, 'My Lord and my God!'

"Jesus said to him, 'Because you have seen Me, have you believed?' " (John 20:19-29 NASB).

A professor of history is teaching his course at a state university. He is saying, "The code of Hammurabi predates the code of Moses and probably Moses did not get the law as the Bible says he did. He probably copied the law from other sources. To frighten the people of Israel into obedience, he took the tablets of stone up the mountain and came down with the tablets, saying that God had carved the laws in the stone with His finger.

When one student asks, "What about the smoke and fire on the mountain," the professor laughs and says, "That was probably a convenient violent thunderstorm with a lot of brilliant lightning."

In the back of the room is Susie Harris, a freshman from Dillsboro, Georgia. Susie has been reared in the Bible Belt. She has been going to church as long as she can remember. She has always been a "good girl." She believes the Bible just as it was written, word for word. She wears a pin for ten years of perfect attendance in Sunday school. She has a religion of rules. It makes no difference what the rules are. The rules can be the Ten Commandments. But her rules might just be the good advice her parents constantly gave her, "Be a good girl." Now, the words of the professor have absolutely shattered her. Her religion of rules is suddenly gone. What she believed all of her life is not true.

That night, Susie sits down and writes her mother a

102

letter. "Dear Mom," it says, "I know you will not like to hear this. I am giving up on religion. There is nothing to it. The Bible is not true. I am going to become an atheist. I am giving up religion." Susie is exactly right—she is giving up *religion*—religion is all she ever had. She joined the church, but everything she believed was secondhand from her parents, her church and her culture.

Susie joined the church when she was eight years old. All her friends were doing it. The pastor asked her if she trusted Jesus and she said, "Yes." She had always trusted Jesus. She believed in Jesus just as she had believed in Santa Claus until she was seven years old. She believed in Santa Claus with all her heart. But it was really not that hard to give up faith in Santa Claus because she never knew Santa Claus as a person.

What she really had in her religion was a set of rules and mental assent to the fact that Jesus lived, died and rose again. She knew the facts of the gospel well. She had heard the preachers say that the Bible was the Word of God and that it was truth. The rules she believed in were the ones she had heard all her life: "Go to Sunday school and church on Sunday" and "Be a good girl." There were certain things you didn't do if you were a "nice" girl, and certain things that you did if you were a "good" girl. Suddenly the whole thing is gone in one lecture in a university classroom!

There are millions of people who have tried one brand of religion or another and have given them up. Their religious faith was shed like a shabby old coat and never put on again. The reasons for throwing away our religion can be moral, religious or social. We start climbing the social ladder and our old religious faith is hardly fashionable in the society we now move in. A moral lapse reveals our weakness and we just give up on religion. We discover that something we believed in with childlike faith is not true and we just "chuck the whole thing."

Whatever the reason, most adults in America who are not attending religious services had some kind of religion in the past that they gave up. Religion is like politics—you can change it as you need it. It is much more difficult to give up religion when it is an important part of a culture and that culture is closed. In an open society, such as we have in America, where different races and cultures are intermingling, interacting, and intermarrying, it is not very difficult at all.

When Susie's mother read her letter, she probably berated her husband for not setting a good example for Susie in his church attendance. Then she probably wrote the university a hot letter for letting atheists teach classes. Finally, she probably called the pastor, told him the story and said she didn't think she could "face anyone at the church any more." Susie's mother didn't know how easy it was for her daughter to give up her religion in the new setting of university life. Probably Susie had already been having some doubts about the "no drinking" and "no sex without marriage" rules. The professor's words gave her an opportunity to shed "the shabby old coat." It really didn't hurt much and it may have been a relief.

Why are so many people disappointed with religion? They are not against it; they are just tired of it. They are not antagonistic, only apathetic. They no longer care. The two large groups of unevangelized people in the United States are the pagans and the apostatized (those who have left their faith). It may well be that the first group are more open to the new birth than the second. It is highly probable that, in the United States, the apostatized outnumber the pagans three to one. This is true because of our strong religious history and because most immigrants brought some kind of religion with them. All of this emphasizes that there are millions like Susie who have given up religion and that is all they had to give up.

But there is more, so much more, to a real living relationship with Jesus Christ as a person whom we know and love. The new birth makes us alive to God in such a real way that He becomes as real to us as our natural parents. Susie never knew a person as Savior and Lord. One can give up a system of beliefs rather easily under the right circumstances, as we have shown. But one does not give up that easily on a person. Being a Christian is not a religion. It is a way of life. It is life in Christ. Religion crucified Jesus Christ and He did not come to establish another religion. Christianity is Christ. It is knowing Jesus Christ in a new birth of faith, hope and love. Being a Christian is not obeying Christian ethics and observing Christian morality. It is not "doing good" or "being good." It is not observing the demands of a Christian culture. "You must be born again." It is not a doctrine, it is an experience. It is not growing into Christian ways, it is a dramatic change of direction from going our way, to going His way. It is not our decision to do something; it is His finding us, in our need.

We do not give up a person we know as easily as we do a set of rules or a religious belief. I was not aware of my first birth, but someone would have a difficult time convincing me that my father was not "for real." My relationship with him was not based on my faith in a birth certificate or because I understood all the mysteries of physical birth. I knew my father as a person. His relationship to me was that of father. Our relationship to God in Jesus Christ in a second birth is similar.

I do not have a relationship to the Father in Jesus Christ because the Bible says so. I do not have that relationship because I understand all the mysteries of spiritual birth. That relationship is a result of real personal experience with Jesus Christ in which God

105

became real to me, a loving Father. Living in that relationship causes me to experience daily the Father's care and love. This is what Susie did not have and so could not give up. Religion that is a set of rules or a philosophy of life can be modified or even given up rather easily under the right circumstances. A faith born out of a personal experience with God is not so easily shaken.

A great deal of religious faith never gets beyond faith in a traditional God. It is possible to believe in such a God, but it does not affect our behavior in the least. It has already been mentioned that religion crucified Jesus Christ, but the crucifiers had no mercy. They were like rapacious dogs in their cruelty. The complaint is often heard that, though church membership continues to grow, it has very little effect on private and public morality and behavior. This is a valid complaint and a valid charge against religion.

I recently saw some of the pictures of Mars that were taken by Mariner II. I saw the pictures. I believed that they came from Mars. But believing that fact did not alter my behavior. I had no emotional response to it. I was intellectually interested. I believed it. It did not change my life in the least. This is the way many people believe in the traditional God. And there is nothing wrong with this if it leads us to experience God as a person in Jesus Christ, and to a new birth. This is true about the revelation of God in the Bible. The Bible really is just the history of people who had an experience with God. The New Testament is the record of how people came to know and experience Jesus Christ as God. We can believe all those stories and it does not affect us one way or another. It is history, much like the history of our country, with stories about great men. That is exactly what the Bible is to many religious people; they accept it as fact, but it has no effect on their lives.

The new birth is an experience with the God of the

Bible in which He comes alive to us in Jesus Christ. Each person has this experience and it is personal. There is no standard scenario for the experience. Two experiences from the New Testament itself are very different. Saul of Tarsus was going to Damascus to persecute Christians when he saw a light so bright he was blinded for several days. He heard Jesus asking him why he was persecuting Him. He found refuge in the house of Judas the Tanner in Damascus and there was taught in the Christian faith by a disciple (Acts 9:1-19). Alternatively, John, the Beloved, relates his experience with Jesus Christ (I John 1:1-4) as "touching Him" and "handling Him" and "seeing Him" and "hearing Him." He recalls no lights, no visions.

The important thing is that they both had an experience with God in Jesus Christ. From that time on, they knew Him personally. What they knew affected their lives. Paul never persecuted anyone after that. John's whole life was one of love. Critics of the Christian faith point out that Christians have done some terrible things, including waging war, conducting inquisitions, torturing people and committing other atrocities too horrible to think about. Believing in a traditional God and using the name "Christian" does not make one a true Christian. *You must be born again.* Isaac Watts was a church member, a "Christian," slave-trading sea captain, but, when he was born again, he quit the slave trade and joined efforts to stop it. His experiential faith affected his whole life.

John Wesley's life, because of the detail of his journals, is an open book and a commentary on the need for experiential faith in God. This man is no great sinner saved from the fires of hell. He is a churchman par excellence. Everyone who knew him would have said that he was a model Christian. Yet there were some serious deficiencies in his life and character. If one had asked John Wesley, before his experiences in Georgia, if he believed in God, he would have said, "Of course, I believe in God. I am a priest of the Church of England. I have spent my life preparing to serve Him. Yes, I believe in God." He believed in God, but God was not real to him. The Christians he knew and served in Georgia disowned him. The girl he fell in love with turned her back on him. He appeared in court several times. He had to flee Georgia like a common criminal. In the days when the chips were down, the God he believed in was not able to help him. John Wesley felt a need for and sought a God whom he knew and could trust. In the new birth at Aldersgate, he found God in Jesus Christ. It was a different John Wesley who breathed new fire into the dying embers of the church that hated him and cast him out. He needed a God of whom he could say, "This is my God." No man since Paul ever did so much or paid so high a price for his experiential faith in Jesus Christ as John Wesley.

Millenniums before John Wesley, Job believed in a God of tradition. His God was one who blessed you if you did what was right and withhheld his blessings if you did not live right. Job went on trusting God until life got tough and he had lost everything he loved and worked for. The man Job, probably living in Idumea or Arabia centuries before our Lord was born, agonized in his tragedy. Friends who shared his faith in the God of tradition were no help, and finally Job almost despaired of ever finding God. His wife urged him to give up and die. Then, out of his need and desperation, Job cried out to God for understanding and mercy. He found God in an experience of faith, a God who was real and loving. After peace came, Job said to God, in beautiful poetry:

> *I know, Lord, that you are all-powerful;*
> *that you can do everything you want.*
> *You ask how I dare question your wisdom*
> *when I am so very ignorant.*

I talked about things I did not understand,
about marvels too great for me to know.
You told me to listen while you spoke
and to try to answer your questions.
Then I knew only what others had told me,
but now I have seen you with my own eyes.
So I am ashamed of all I have said
and repent in dust and ashes.

(Job 42:2-6 TEV)

Doubting Thomas

Thomas, "the Twin," so skeptical before his religious experience when he cried out, "My Lord and my God," could very well be the patron saint of Susie and millions like her. He believed desperately in the mission of Jesus. His courage cannot be called into question. When Lazarus was lying on his deathbed, word of his illness came to Jesus. The holy band determined that they would go to Bethany. They well knew this might mean death for Jesus, because hatred against Him had become enormous in the capital. Bethany often housed hundreds of Passover pilgrims and word would be sure to get to the authorities that Jesus was near. When the decision was made, it was Thomas who said, "Let's go with Him and die with Him" (John 11:16).

In the upper room, where Jesus spent the last hours of His life with His men, Jesus said, "You know where I am going, and you know the way." Thomas should have known. Jesus had been teaching them about His kingdom of love.

But Thomas blurted out, "Lord, we do not know where you are going and how can we know the way?"

Jesus gave the great answer, "I am the way, the truth, and the life, and no one comes to the Father

109

except by me" (John 14:1-6). Thomas needs to know that Jesus is not just a great teacher of the way, but He is the way. He does not just speak the truth about God, He is the truth of God. He is not just telling men about a way of life, He is life.

Thomas is really not a name at all but means "twin." Didymus also means "twin" in the Greek language. Tradition says that he was "Judas, the twin" to distinguish him from the two other men named Judas. Tradition has also given him the label of Doubting Thomas. There is more faith in honest doubt than in many creeds worn slick with repetition. For Thomas, it was easy to believe in the flesh-and-blood Jesus. He believed in the sincerity he saw deep in His eyes. He believed in the dream of the Kingdom of God. But that all ended on a bloody cross outside Jerusalem. Thomas said, "He died. I saw Him die. I will never believe until I can put my fingers in the wounds in His hands, His feet and His side." He wants to see and feel. He will trust only what his senses tell him.

What can we really believe in? Can we believe in gold that creates but never satisfies hunger? Can we believe in land that ultimately will give us only a space two and a half by six feet? Can we believe in glory that is a fading mirage of a millisecond in the endlessness of eternity? Can we trust flesh that ends corrupting in the grave? Are these the things we must have in order to live fully? "You only go around once in life." Are these the things to which we can give ourselves to wring the most out of life?

Christ invites us to get started on a daring adventure into the supernatural. A supernatural God has revealed Himself in a supernatural person, the God-man, Jesus Christ, our Savior and Lord. Jesus Christ spoke into existence a supernatural body, the church. The only way one can experience this body and join the family of God is through a supernatural birth. *You must be born again.* The just do not live by bread or wealth or power, but by faith. The new birth enables us to see the invisible, believe the incredible and do the impossible. Given new faculties, we see in the darkness, hear in the silence and feel His presence in the solitude. This is impossible for earthbound creatures. The faith which it takes to believe this is the gift of God. The point at which God meets us is that point where we can no longer stand the darkness and the silence and the solitude. Then we reach out for someone beyond ourselves.

Jesus gave us an illustration of this very point in Luke 16:19-31. The parable, on its face, is a complete enigma. Here was a man whose style of life included eating well and having fine linen next to the skin and rich purple for an outer garment. What's wrong with that? He was rich. What's wrong with that? There is no hint that he was a sexual deviate or a moral wretch. He did not get his wealth by deceit or trickery. He did not pull a Watergate "break-in" or make illegal campaign contributions. But he went to hell. For what? Other people have desired more luxurious clothing. Other people have been guilty of overeating.

On the other hand, Lazarus was a poor wretch, a beggar. He had nothing. We are not told that he joined the church. We are not told that he was born again. We are not told that he had excellent character. He died and went to heaven. Why? On the surface it appears that this is an excellent gospel for the communists. All the rich people are going to hell and all the poor people are going to heaven?

The key to the parable is that, in the case of the rich man, the sum total of his whole life was in what he ate and what he wore. He believed that what you taste in your mouth and what you feel on your skin are the only realities. He was unmoved by compassion for the beggar at his gate, because hell is lovelessness. It is people like this who go to hell. On the other hand, Lazarus had nothing except his name. The name of a person was very important in Jewish history and story-telling, and Lazarus means "God is my helper." He had nothing except his need for God. It is people like that who go to heaven.

Jesus was saying to the Pharisees, "who were lovers of money" (Luke 16:14), that it is not what we eat or what we wear that is important. What is important is that we seek first the Kingdom of God (Matthew 6:32,33). Only one thing can bring us to God and that is our need for Him. God does not inevitably call to salvation the logicians or the powerful or the noble born. Because of this, no one can boast that he deserves salvation. It is by "His doing" that we are saved and Christ has become "wisdom and righteousness" for us and in Him we are put right with God (justified) and made part of God's own people (sanctified) and set free (redeemed) (I Corinthians 1:26-31).

The Missing Link

What did Thomas miss on that first evening, when Jesus appeared to the disciples? He missed a personal experience with the risen Lord. He missed seeing Him alive. We don't know why he was absent. Perhaps he had given it all up, including his religion. All of his dreams had been shattered on a skull-shaped hill. It was a great dream while it lasted, but it was all over now.

Some of the disciples probably continued to meet in the upper room where they had heard His last great words. They must have met in terror, as the hatred of the religious leaders was at a boiling point. The fact that they continued to meet is a testimony to their courage. Every step on the stairs and every knock on

112

the door could have meant the Sanhedrin had decreed their death. Suddenly, one evening, Jesus was right there among them. He gave them the greeting that they had heard so often, "Peace be to you." He held out His hands and they saw the wounds. He drew back His garment and they saw the riven side. Their hearts were filled with joy as the overwhelming knowledge that He was alive began to seep into their brains. Right had triumphed over wrong. Love had triumphed over hate. Life had triumphed over death. He was alive!

The world is not yet through with that bloody man who hung between heaven and earth on that "green hill far way without the city wall." He lives. He is still an issue with us. Franklin Roosevelt was a man over whom controversy raged while he was living. Roosevelt is dead and there is no controversy over him today. Only very few scholars argue the point (and then without passion) as to whether he was a social messiah or the tool of the very rich. Hitler was an issue in the 1930s and 1940s. Men hated him fanatically or followed him blindly. Hitler is dead and is no longer an issue. Napoleon was an issue while he lived. Was he the author of the "Grand Design" for Europe or a mad dictator? Napoleon is dead and men no longer fight over him.

But Jesus Christ remains an issue. A self-proclaimed atheist was very vocal in ridiculing the Christian faith and, on one occasion, said at a gathering, "I have dedicated my life to proving there is nothing to Christianity and nothing to Christ. Christ was a faker, a cheap magician who confused country bumpkins, and anyone who believes in Him is a fool."

A man who had been quietly listening asked him, "You mean that you believe there is nothing to Christianity and to Jesus Christ?"

He replied, "Absolutely nothing."

The man said, "You are an educated man and you

113

claim to have great learning, and yet you have dedicated your life to fighting nothing!"

Because He lives, He is an issue in every nation of the world.

Thomas not only missed seeing our Lord alive; he missed the benediction of peace. Not as a salutation, but as a gift, Christ said, "Peace be with you." On another occasion, our Lord talked about the peace that He gives. He had said, perhaps in that same room earlier, "I give you my peace. I give you a peace that the world cannot give. Do not allow your heart to be troubled or afraid" (John 14:27).

The source of all peace is peace with God. It is wonderful to be right with your neighbors, your teachers, your parents and your friends. But it is even more basic to be at peace with God. Trouble and fear are the twin ghosts of modern man. The new birth is a new birth of peace. How can we understand the problem of war when we do not understand why we cannot get along with our own families? Our violent society is a testimony to the need for inner peace. An experience with the risen Lord is the sure knowledge that right is stronger than wrong, love is stronger than hate, life is stronger than death. That assurance relieves us of the need to strike out at society, our friends and those we love, in anger and frustration. We know how the story ends. We have met Him "who is our peace and who has made us, both Jew and Gentile, one, and has broken down the walls of anger and frustration that were between us" (Ephesians 2:14). John Masefield, in "The Everlasting Mercy," has Saul Kane recount his experience with Christ:

> *I did not think, I did not strive,*
> *The deep peace burned me alive;*
> *The bolted door had broken in,*
> *I knew that I had done with sin.*

114

I knew that Christ had given me birth
  To brother all the souls on earth,
And every bird and every beast
  Should share the crumbs broke at the feast.

Thomas missed the commission of our Lord, "as the Father has sent me, I also send you" (John 20:21). He sends those who have encountered the living Lord in experiential faith on mission. The mission is His mission. It is the same mission on which the Father sent Him. It is a mission into danger. Without Him, it is a "mission impossible." His work was never completed. He gave His whole life to creating followers who would bring His mission to completion.

The new birth is the beginning of following in his steps, doing what He did, saying what He said, loving as He loved. There is no "cheap grace." In Luke 14, He revealed three conditions for discipleship. The disciple cannot be possessed by others. "If anyone come to Me, and does not hate his own father and mother and wife and children and brothers and sisters, yes, and even his own life, he cannot be My disciple." (Luke 14:26) The disciple cannot be possessed by self. "Whoever does not carry his own cross and come after Me cannot be My disciple" (Luke 14:27). The disciple cannot be possessed by things. "So, therefore, no one of you can be My disciple who does not give up all his own possessions" (Luke 14:33). Discipleship is belonging to Jesus Christ by resurrection, His and ours. Loyalty to Him and His mission supersedes all the demands of family, self and things.

His peace and His resurrection! Thomas missed the things that relate a person to God. These are "missing links" in so many lives. Religion and good works cannot relate one to God in such a way that His peace is a present possession. The empty tomb is the grave of all our troubles and fears. The legacy of His death and resurrection is peace. Horatius Bonar said it well:

I change, He changes not,
  The Christ can never die;
His love, not mine, the resting-place,
  His truth, not mine, the tie.
The cross still stands unchanged,
  Though heaven is now His home;
The mighty stone is rolled away,
  But yonder is His tomb.

And yonder is my peace,
  The grave of all my woes;
I know the Son of God has come,
  I know He died and rose.
I know He liveth now
  At God's right hand above;
I know the throne on which He sits,
  I know His truth and love.

Thomas missed the experience of being empowered by the Holy Spirit. Christ will not send disciples on mission alone. In that same room, He had already introduced them to the Helper (John 14:26). The Risen Lord tells the church to "wait in Jerusalem" for the power of the Spirit before they set out on mission into danger, death and discouragement (Luke 24:49). In the new birth, the believer is "sealed with the Holy Spirit of promise" (Ephesians 1:13). The Holy Spirit is the earnest (down payment) of the inheritance in Christ. At the moment of birth, the infant has all the possibilities and capabilities for a healthy, normal life. The infant, however, needs helpers— parents, teachers and others—to assist in living up to these possibilities and capabilities.

There is a parallel here with what happened in the creation account in Genesis. God breathed into man the breath of life and he became a living soul (Genesis 2:7). Jesus breathed on them and said, "Receive the Holy Spirit" (John 20:22). The coming of the Holy

Spirit to a life "dead in trespasses and sins" (Ephesians 2:1) is a creation. It is life from the dead. It is a new birth. When the leaders of the early church were arrested, warned and then released, they return to their witnessing and the authorities seized them again and asked them why they were so stubborn. They said, "We are witnesses of these things and so is the Holy Spirit whom God has given to those who are obedient to Him" (Acts 5:25-32). They were saying that they were not alone. The Holy Spirit, the Helper, was with them, helping them to know what to say and do. The gift of the Holy Spirit is the birthright and birthgift of every believer.

Thomas missed the responsibility. Jesus told the disciples, when Thomas was absent, that they had power and responsibility. Because the message was in their hands, the spiritual life and death of others would depend on their loyalty and faithfulness. If they withheld the message of God's forgiving love, people would not hear. If they shared the message, people would hear and believe. In this sense, they had power to forgive or not forgive sin. If people are to be forgiven, they must know the Forgiver. Only those who have known the joy of sin forgiven can share the knowledge of the Forgiver.

The gospel of the new birth is news that we cannot keep to ourselves. It demands to be shared. This is the responsibility of every born again Christian. One of the conclusions of the Gallup poll on born again Christians, released in September of 1976, was, "The greater missionary zeal of the evangelical group of churches may be an important reason why these churches are experiencing a spectacular growth in membership while certain mainline churches are experiencing serious membership losses." The poll reported that a much higher proportion of people in the evangelical groups reported a born again experience.

The "missing links" in the lives of people are the

117

links that can relate us to God in a new birth. The experience of knowing a living Lord, the possession of His peace, the sense of being on His mission, and the empowering of the Holy Spirit can make "new creatures" out of "just church members." Thomas missed all of these things because he did not have the personal experience with the Lord risen from the dead. These are the things that Thomas missed on that evening when he was absent from the fellowship. He was not there because he had given up on religion. The day after that fellowship meeting, the testimony of those present was that "we have seen the Lord." It was then that he said he would never believe unless his fingers could feel the wounds and his hands could touch the riven side. It was their testimony that brought him back again the next week to the meeting of the fellowship. It is that simple testimony of rebirth that awakens hearts to their need of Him. The testimony of changed lives which have touched Him and have been touched by Him is more effective than great choirs or great preachers.

The Validity of Experience

When the disciples met again, Thomas was present. They talked about Jesus for some time. They recalled for one another the things He had said and the things He had done. Thomas only waited. Then He was among them. He greeted them, as they commonly greeted one another, with the "shalom" of Israel. His eyes went right to Thomas. "Come, Thomas," he said, "Put your fingers in the wounds in my hands and feet. Reach out to Me and put your hand in my riven side. Do not be filled with unbelief. Believe Me, trust Me. (John 20:26,27) Thomas looked into the eyes of

Christ, saw the love and compassion and, falling down before Him, cried, "My Lord and my God." Now he could say, "This is my God." In all the history of man, at any given time, only some have known the ecstasy of that discovery. David, centuries before Christ, made that great discovery and said:

> O God, you are my God
> and I long for you.
> My whole being desires you;
> like a dry, worn-out, and waterless land,
> my soul is thirsty for you.
> Let me see you in the sanctuary;
> let me see how mighty and glorious you are.
> Your constant love is better than life itself,
> and so I will praise you.

> (Psalms 63:1-3 TEV)

Thomas does not put his fingers in the wounds in His hands. He does not place his hand in the riven side. Now he knows that there is a level of knowledge beyond the five senses. He is no longer earthbound. Now he rises above the animal perceptions and sees as a man (*anthropos*) made to walk upright and look into the face of God. Now God is real to him in Jesus Christ. God does not speak, but we hear Him. He has no form for our eyes, but we see Him. He has no physical body, but we touch Him.

Those who claim to know God in this way today, to know Him as Thomas came to know Him, as "my Lord, and my God," are found among many Christian denominations. Knowing God personally in a new birth is not the possession of any denomination or group. In September of 1976, Jimmy Carter, who was to become President of the United States, testified to a new birth. This focused the attention of the press on this religious experience. The Gallup poll of September 1976 was a result of this interest. The first question in the poll was, "Would you say that you have been 'born again' or have had a 'born again' experience—that is, a turning point in your life when you committed yourself to Christ?" Here are the results nationwide and by key groups:

Have you had a "born again" experience?

Nationwide	34%
Protestants	48%
Catholics	18%
Men	28%
Women	39%
College	27%
High School	36%
Grade School	42%
18–29 years	29%
30–49 years	33%
50 and over	39%
East	23%
Midwest	34%
South	55%
West	20%

A personal relationship with God in Jesus Christ through a born again experience is not something claimed by only a few persons in a few denominations in an isolated part of our country. The high figures among youth are related to the spiritual revival among young people that has been going on since the "Jesus Revolution" in the early 1970s. However, the second highest percentage goes to the "over fifty" age group. Although Protestants show a significantly higher percentage, almost one out of every five Catholics claims to have been born again.

The experience of the new birth is not the exclusive claim of any one denomination or group of Christians. It is an experience found with significant frequency among mainline denominations and among the newer, more recently formed denominations and groups. The new birth is something that has happened in the lives of thirty-four per cent of our youth and adults. This, in itself, is a testimony to the validity of this experience. Although it is outside of the purview of the poll, from personal experience with thousands who have been born again in the United States, Europe, Canada, the Caribbean and the South Pacific, I know that thousands of these people found victory over alcoholism, drug addiction, homosexuality, worry and fear, through this experience. Others did not have those kinds of problems but found inner peace and certainty.

The new birth has been tested and proven in the laboratory of human experience. It is something that millions of persons have testified to in every generation since Jesus Christ walked this earth. If anything were tested in a laboratory and positive results were obtained in such a large percentage of test animals or humans, it could be said that it was tested and found valid. The fact that the mysteries of the new birth are not understood has nothing to do with its validity. Thousands of things are done and used every day for which science has no explanation. If they work, use them. Millions have been born again and have come to know God personally in their experience. That experience is both authoritative and valid. I am an expert on what has happened to me. You are an expert on what has happened to you. No one can refute the religious, social, moral and ethical changes in a person who has a new relationship to God in the new birth. We have not put off first births just because everything about them is not understood. Why deny the new birth because all the mysteries of spiritual birth are not understood?

The validity of the spiritual experience of rebirth is also witnessed to by the way it communicates. The lay person in the church has great difficulty communicating Christian theology. A case in point is the virgin birth of our Lord. If Christians hang their case for

Jesus Christ on His virgin birth, they are obligated "to prove" that He was in fact born of a virgin. There is no way that any theologian or lay person can prove the "mystery of incarnation." What usually results is a hot argument with an unbeliever that does neither the believer nor the unbeliever any good and may do both a lot of harm. The case for Christ must be based on what has happened to me. If nothing has happened, then one has no case. It is just that simple.

An effective witness says, "Bill, I cannot argue with you about religion. I cannot answer all the questions you have about where Cain got his wife or whether or not the whale really swallowed Jonah. Let me share with you what has happened to me, what God has done in my life. I had a lot of problems. I was trying to work them out myself but there was no way, man. I had a friend who told me what Jesus Christ had done for him. I knew I needed something. I tried everything but nothing worked until this friend came along. I gave Jesus Christ my life. Man, it was like a different world. I know now that I was born again. I am not perfect, Bill, but, man, am I different. Things are really working out at home now. Doris and I are getting along fine. I love her more than I ever did. The kids are behaving better. I am spending more time with them. Jesus is helping me to live everyday one day at a time for Him. It's great, Bill, and I wish you would try it." That communicates because it is valid testimony, not argument.

The validity of the experience of rebirth is related to how recently the experience took place. People are neither impressed by nor interested in a stale experience. Some people relate their experience with God in Christ and it is all about something that happened long ago. The test for validity is pragmatic—if it works, it's true and, if it's true, it works. Does the experience relate to everyday life? Is it helping with interpersonal relationships in the home and at work? Does it offer relief from trouble and fear? Does it affect behavior?

122

Experiences related in terms of emotion and the past without relating the experience to the concerns of everyday life and the common problems of life elicit very little desire to share the experience. The church is really the "church of what's happening now." The new birth is just that, a birth—the beginning of life. Its validity is not based upon the fact that it was a sensational spiritual experience from the past but upon its claim on the whole person and all relationships now.

The whole matter of the Christian life is a matter of living a life worth sharing and sharing a life worth living. The life that you now have in Christ, is it worth sharing? Would you want everyone to have the same quality of life you now have? Many religious people are not excited about sharing their faith because they really have nothing to share. There is nothing exciting about sharing a baptismal certificate or a creed that you subscribed to. When faith in Jesus Christ is a "love affair" that is going on right now, that is exciting and satisfying and it is not difficult for people to want to share it. It is never easy to share "bad news," but it is hard to hoard "good news." The gospel is the good news about the meanings that His love and care have for us right now.

The God of Experience

The experience of new birth is an experience with Jesus Christ. In Him we discover what God is like. Jesus never once discussed the existence of God. He never verbalized the familiar and very ineffective "proofs" for the existence of God. You never hear Him use the clever little illustrations (such as the watch and the watchmaker) that are supposed to demonstrate clearly the existence of God. The concepts of theology

123

about "general revelation" and "special revelation" evidently never crossed His mind. It was not just that He lived in a society that took the existence of God for granted. It was more than that. He possessed a quiet level of faith in which every breath He drew, every word He spoke, every act He did was drawn and spoken and acted in the light of the fact of God. A life well lived, whose every move and word and deed is a clear convincing testimony to the fact of God, convinces more sinners than all the books of theology that have ever been written.

It is natural that since we meet God in a personal way in the new birth, that we should discover in the experience of birth that God is a Father. In our first glimpse of the young man Jesus, at the age of twelve, we hear Him saying to His anxious mother, "Don't you understand that I must be about the work of My Father?" (Luke 2:49). Twenty years later, we see the bloody man on a cross and, if we come close to His dying agony, we can hear Him barely whisper, "Father, into your hands I place My Spirit" (Luke 23:46). His whole life was an exposition of God as a loving Father. The most graphic and beautiful parable that He tells is the parable of the waiting father in Luke 15. When Jesus wants to tell us what God is like, He tells us that He is a Father who loves. Indeed, in this one story, Jesus tells us what God is like, what sin is like, what repentance is like, what forgiveness is like, what self-righteousness is like and what salvation is like. In simple, moving language, Jesus, in just about six hundred words, tells us more about God, salvation, forgiveness and love than any one hundred books of theology ever written. Almost everything that Jesus tells us about the Father is in the terms of the family and other human relationships. There are some occasional references to God as Father in the Old Testament, but they cannot approach the clear way that Jesus reveals God as "His Father" and "our Father."

The most revolutionary and explosive fact ever revealed is that God is a Father. It means that behind and above all the mysterious forces of our universe, and all the agonies and ecstasies of man's life upon planet earth, are the wise and loving purposes of the Father. He is the God and Father of our Lord Jesus Christ and our Father in Jesus Christ, and He is in control. There is meaning in the mosaic of agony and ecstasy that is human life. He is so much better than people can ever comprehend. No earthly father, no matter how good, can approach the goodness of God. "If you, being human, know how to give good gifts to your children, how much more shall the heavenly Father give the Holy Spirit to those who ask Him?" (Luke 11:13). He is not some kind of "goodness concept" or "goodness principle," but He is goodness acting graciously on behalf of His children. Paul, speaking to the impenitent man, appeals to the goodness of God as one of the things that should lead man to repentance: "Do you treat lightly His rich kindness, His putting up with you, and His patience? Don't you know that the goodness of God should lead you to repentance?" (Romans 2:4). To respond to the goodness of God by faith is to come to know God as Father.

To discover God as Father in the new birth is to discover man, my brother. He is the "Father of us all," even those who do not want Him. The worth and dignity of the human person comes alive as God is our Father. There is something seriously wrong with man in the core of his being. Nothing else can explain the Hitlers, the Manson clan, the devil worshipers, the murderers, the rapists, or the beast that rages in the best of us. Down deep in man, there are chords broken and crushed by something evil and diabolic. But, if touched by the loving heart of God and wakened by the goodness of God, they can vibrate with the harmony of the holy once again. It is a "cop out" for us to say we are just "the naked ape" reverting to the jungle. If

125

that is true, then we must kill all those who have such tendencies and let planned selection evolve a new race of men. Our only prospect then is Aldous Huxley's "brave new world." To discover that we are sons of God by a new birth is to discover that man is infinitely worth saving. No man is so far away from God that He cannot come home. Augustine said, "He loves us as though there were but one of us to love." Racism and apartheid are obscene to the new man in Christ. All the barriers that separate man from man must be crossed in self-denying love to reach and free our brothers lost to His goodness, and their dignity as sons of God.

To know God as Father by spiritual birth is to come to know and experience the community of believers. He teaches us to pray, "Our Father" (Matthew 6:9). He is not only the Father of all men by creation; He is, in a special sense, the Father of His community of faith. In the new birth we have been refathered. Jesus spoke of the fatherhood of God in three different ways. Essentially, God is the Father of Jesus Christ. Peculiarly, God is the Father of His community. Inclusively, He is the Father of all men. Only those who have been born again can know Him in all three of these ways. To know God peculiarly is to know Him as the Father of His own people, the new community. To know God essentially is to know Him in His relationship to Jesus Christ. The word "father" is not related so much to the origin of our spiritual life as it is to the nourishment of our spiritual life. He is the One who nourishes and sustains the life of the spiritual community. As Father to the community, He watches over it (providence); He cares for it; He thinks about it; He guides it; He gifts it. Knowing Him as Father, the community is encouraged to make real in loving community His love. The loving community on earth is a reflection of that loving eternal community which is God who has revealed Himself to us as Father, Son and Holy Spirit.

The experience of knowing God as loving Father in new birth is to have assurance of life after death. It is to have eternal life. "These things Jesus spoke; and lifting up His eyes to heaven, He said, 'Father, the hour has come; glorify Thy Son, that the Son may glorify Thee, even as Thou gavest Him authority over all mankind, that to all whom Thou has given Him, He may give eternal life. And this is eternal life, that they may know Thee, the only true God, and Jesus Christ whom Thou hast sent" (John 17:1-3 NASB).

To believe that everything we are and everything we have begun will someday end forever is unthinkable to many minds. Here again, all arguments are useless. Unless there is a plan and a Planner behind it all, eternal life is only the humorous egotism of vain man. But there is a plan and a Planner and it is the plan of the Father. "Blessed be the God and Father of our Lord Jesus Christ, who has blessed us with every spiritual blessing in the heavenly places in Christ . . . with a view to the administration suitable to the fulness [completion] of the times, that is, the summing up of all things in Christ, things in the heavens and things upon the earth" (Ephesians 1:3,10 NASB).

Blaise Pascal was born in 1623. His scientific work on the problems of the vacuum won him recognition as a scientist in 1648. His work on calculus and cycloid curves won him recognition as a mathematician. He became deeply interested in man's relationship to God. He was especially unhappy with the traditional relationship of man to God in the doctrines of the church. His work, *Lettres Provencales,* advocated a spiritual and personal approach to God. It put great stress on man's union with the mystical body of Christ through love. His "prayer of conversion" deeply affected John Wesley later.

Actually, Pascal represents the roots of the evangelical awakening that shook two continents a century later. Near the close of 1654, he had reached a crisis in his search for a meaningful relationship with God. And, then, one night, he had a religious experience which changed his life. The account of that experience, which Pascal called "the night of fire," was carefully written on parchment and sewn into the lining of his coat. Until the day of his death, he wore that coat as a constant reminder of that night. The parchment inscription ended, "Forgetfulness of the world, and all except God. He is to be found only in the ways taught in the gospel. Greatness of the human soul. O righteous Father, the world hath not known Thee, but I have known Thee."

This is the certainty of experience. Neither the traditions of the church and its traditional God nor its theology can give you this inner certainty which you long for and seek. It is received only in a personal encounter with Jesus Christ who is the way to the Father.

It was different, and you can say that again. Who would ever believe that I was in a church today? I'll say one thing for Jerry, he never gives up. The surprising thing is that I really like the guy. He's for real. I never thought I would say that about any Christian. He is so honest. I guess the most surprising thing is that I liked being in church. It was so different—not at all like I thought it would be. They were so friendly. They were really glad to have me. They acted like I really belonged there. I wonder if they knew the kind of person I am?

I liked that small sharing group. They were all so open and honest, especially the girl who talked so freely about her problem. It was so good the way they all gathered around her and prayed for her. I really wished that I might have shared my problem with them. When that guy talked about his doubts, they didn't get mad and argue. Some others even admitted they had doubts sometimes. It was really good.

Come to think of it, they were kind of like a family, a good family. They were not like my family. They were like what I think a family ought to be. They really cared about each other. I saw tears in the eyes of several of the girls in the sharing group when they were praying for that girl. It couldn't have been an act. I wonder if God has a family.

6.

THE FAMILY OF GOD

"Who do you say that I am?" Jesus asked His disciples. Simon Peter said, "You are the Christ, the Son of the living God." Jesus said to Peter, "You are blessed, Peter, for you did not get that answer from man, but from the heavenly Father. I tell you that you are Peter and upon this rock I will build My church and not even the gates of the grave will be able to stand against it" (Matthew 16:16-18).

"And God placed everything under his rule and appointed him as head over everything for the church which is His body, the completion of Him, who completes everything in every way" (Ephesians 1:22,23).

"As a result of this [the message of peace that was preached to both Jew and Gentile and made them one in His body, the church—Ephesians 2:17-18] you are no longer strangers and foreigners, but fellow citizens with God's people and members of God's family" (Ephesians 2:19).

The living body, the church, the family of God comes into being because of the common experience each member has with Jesus Christ. This living body

131

makes real the love of God and the love of men in the
world. The new birth is a birth into a family. When
Christ draws people to Himself, He draws them to one
another. The body, the family of God, derives its life
from Jesus Christ. Jesus and all the New Testament
writers refer to the church in two ways. In Matthew
16:18, He is speaking of the church as all born again
Christians everywhere. In Matthew 18:17, He speaks
of the church as a local group of born again Christians.
The church must, of necessity, have an organization in
a local community. It is possible that some people
who are members of the organization are really not a
part of the family of God for they have not been born
again. They do not know Jesus Christ as Lord and
Savior experientially. The church, by proclaiming
Christ and the necessity of the new birth, can assist
people to know Christ in this living way. One can point
out that Judas was one of the first disciples and that
Ananias and Sapphira had joined themselves to the
congregation (Acts 5:1-11). Belonging to the church is
not being born again. Through the first birth, one
becomes a member of a family. By the second birth,
one becomes a member of the family of God.

The family of God is called "the people of God,"
which relates in a meaningful way to the purpose of
God in the world. God had a purpose in the people of
Israel. His promise to Abraham was, "I will make you
a great people" (Genesis 12:2). The unfaithfulness of
God's people in the Old Testament did not block the
purpose of God. God has now chosen those who were
not originally a people to be a people, the people of
God. They are the new Israel of God, His people, the
church (Romans 9:24-26). They are now called the
sons of God.

John the Baptist saw himself as a part of the purpose of God in "making ready a prepared people for
the Lord" (Luke 1:17). Paul, in his letter to Titus,
speaks of Christ, "who gave Himself for us, that He

might redeem us from every lawless deed and purify for Himself a people for His own possession, zealous for good deeds" (Titus 2:14 NASB). Paul quotes from the Old Testament as he talks about the kind of lives Christians should live as the body of Christ, "And I will be a Father to you, and you shall be sons and daughters to Me" (II Corinthians 6:18). A decision was made at the Jerusalem conference on the relationship of the ceremonial law of the Old Testament to the new church. James recalls the testimony of Peter, "Simeon has related how God first concerned Himself about taking from among the Gentiles a people for His name" (Acts 15:14). The born again believer is related to the purpose of God in the world through the family of God, the church.

The idea of the family of God as a people has two very deep implications. The first is that the church should carry out the purpose of God in the world through proclamation and ministry. The evangelistic appeal that God is making through His people (II Corinthians 5:19) is impossible unless the appeal is made out of a community of believers. There must be a community to invite others to.

One problem at this point is that the church is identified with a building. People talk of "the church on Twenty-second Street." It ought to be the church that "meets on Twenty-second Street." One does not invite persons to a building or to a meeting, but to a warm, loving fellowship that sets people free (redeems). The new believer, born again, possessing the life of Christ, cannot do without this fellowship, because through it the purpose of God for the world is accomplished.

The second implication of the family of God is that the church is a new creation. It is the creation of a new race of men in which there is no Jew or Gentile, slave or freeman, male or female (Ephesians 3:6; Galatians 3:28). This is God's new social order.

The church has nothing to do with race. It is unfortunate that so many local churches have denied this aspect of the church of the New Testament. The greatest and most stubborn racial barrier in the first-century world was the barrier between Jew and Gentile. It was broken down by Christ and the two races became one new race, the people of God. This new race of men can demonstrate what the world could be like if the world turned to Jesus Christ as Lord. Racial hang-ups, male chauvinism and social distinctions have no place among this people.

The word "church" causes more problems in communication than any other designation for the family of God. Both "people of God" and "family of God" imply a personal relationship with God. The meaning of "church" has gradually become unclear because it is so misused. It is used to indicate a building that has a special use for worship. It is also used to indicate a denomination or group of Christians using some common name, such as Baptist or Methodist.

The problem is that an organization or institution is confused with a people. The word "church" means a "called out assembly." It was used to designate the governing body of the Greek city-state that was "called out" by a herald. The word has a great deal of affinity with the word "saint" which was used to refer to the church by Paul (Ephesians 1:1; Philippians 1:1). The idea is separation, but not in a bad sense. It is not some kind of holier-than-thou separation. It has the meaning of "set apart for a special purpose."

When the New Testament writers referred to the church (the word was used one hundred fifteen times in the New Testament), they were never referring to a denomination or an organizational structure, but to the people of God, either collectively as existing all over the earth, or specifically as a local group of Christians meeting for worship and work. Three times it was used to indicate an assembly that was not Christian (Acts 19). Twice it was used to refer to the people Israel in the Old Testament (Acts 7:38; Hebrews 2:12). All other one hundred ten times it is used in either of the two ways mentioned previously.

Without straining a point it can be said that, out of these two ideas in the Scriptures, two concepts of the church have evolved. One view identifies the church with an institution, a denomination or a group which usually claims that salvation is only found in "The Church." The other is a mystical concept that says that the church is invisible and has no earthly organization and is not "of" (and barely in) this world. Both of these ideas fall seriously short of the New Testament idea about the church and both of them have a serious weakness at the point of impact upon culture.

The institutional church becomes identified with a particular culture and the demands of the gospel become confused with the demands of culture. This was true of the Roman Catholic ethnic churches and it was true of Southern Baptists in the South from the Civil War to the Second World War. Although Southern Baptists abhorred the institutional view of the church, they were caught in a culture trap that got southern culture and the gospel all mixed up. It is strange that the mystical view of a church "that is so heavenly minded it is no earthly good" leads us into the same problem. This view puts the church so above culture, so uninvolved, that it cannot influence culture by being the "light" and "salt" and "leaven" of the gospel. This was true of many of the common life, rural groups of Christians who confused colorful neckties and buttons on dresses with a lack of holiness.

The New Community

What does all this have to do with the new birth? It has a great deal of relevance because the church, the

135

new community, the family of God, the people of God, is not one because it is related to an institution. It is not one because it is related to some mystical invisible congregation halfway between heaven and earth. It is one because it is related to a person, Jesus Christ, and a community of faith composed of real flesh and blood people who are struggling always between what they are and what Christ is teaching them to be.

Their creed is Christ; their theology is John 3:16; their life is incarnating Jesus Christ. They are "in" the world but struggling (with His help) not to be "of" the world. They may or may not be related to a denomination or convention or conference.

There are some concepts about the church in the New Testament that give clues as to the nature of the church and its relationship to culture and the world. Are there some answers on how the church can keep from being "so heavenly minded it is no earthly good" on one hand, and so "earthly minded it is no heavenly good" on the other?

The first concept that gives a clue to the nature of the new community is that it is spiritual. The best word to use here is "charismatic," but in popular thinking today this word is confused with "tongue speaking" or glossolalia.

"Tongues" is one of the charismatic gifts of the Holy Spirit, but it is only one of eleven classifications of gifts. Later in this chapter we will talk about spiritual gifts. The word "charismatic" means simply "of the grace of God." Our salvation, both personal (in the new birth) and corporate (as the body of Christ) is by the grace of God. "For by grace you [the church at Ephesus] have been saved through faith; and that not of yourselves, it is the gift of God" (Ephesians 2:8 NASB). The church is given grace-gifts to assist it in its life and work (I Peter 4:10,11; Ephesians 4:1-16; Romans 12:6-8; I Corinthians 12:14). The church is a living organism with a local body. It has organization

136

to a greater or lesser degree. The organization grows out of the life of the church, but it is not the church.

It is at this point that the new birth is so critical. When the church teaches and preaches the necessity of the new birth it safeguards the spiritual nature of the church. It is possible for people to join the organization when, through self-deception or ignorance, they join the church, though they have never been born again. Joining the organization does not mean they will be a part of the family of God or the people of God. This concept, when faithfully taught and preached, is a constant reminder of the need to be aware of the tension between too close an identification with culture and the need to be involved with culture. This concept reminds the church of the pull from "above."

There is also the pull from "below." The second concept regarding the new community assists the church in an understanding of its relationship to the world around it. The tension is always present between enough involvement to evangelize and to be "salt" and "light" and "leaven" without being neutralized by the religious legalism of the institutional church (which is worldly) and the pagan culture in which we are living. The second concept is that the church as the new community is part of an eternal plan that involves all of God's created order of things. The key to all Bible prophecy and the clue to what God is about in His world is found in the New Testament. "He made known to us the mystery of His will, according to His kind intention which He purposed in Him with a view to an administration suitable to the fulness of the times, that is the summing up of all things in Christ, things in the heavens and things upon the earth" (Ephesians 1:9,10 NASB). Not only is the eternal administrative plan made known, but also the means by which God will carry out His plan. "And to bring to light what is the administration of the mystery [the mystery of the church, His body; see verses 4-6] which for ages has

137

been hidden in God, who created all things; in order that the manifold wisdom of God might now be made known through the church to the rulers and authorities in the heavenly places. This was in accordance with the eternal purpose which He carried out in Christ Jesus our Lord" (Ephesians 3:9-11 NASB). Not only is God going "to get it all together" in Christ, but that administrative plan is in the hands of the church.

This plan concerns God's world. Kings may strut and rattle their sabers; dictators may light their gas ovens for Jews or whomever they hate at the moment; rulers may plan and scheme, carving up nations as though they were pieces of meat; but history is His story and He will write not only the last chapter, but every chapter. The people of God are in on it: Jesus Christ came into the world to redeem (set free) and to reconcile. He says to this church of His, "As the Father has sent me into the world, in the same way I am sending you" (John 20:21). To the seventy that he sent out, He said, "Look, I am sending you out as sheep among wolves" (Matthew 10:16).

The church is on His mission into danger. Christians all pretty much agree on what God wants to do in redeeming and reconciling the world to Himself, but they violently disagree on the timing of it. One group postpones the Kingdom of God until His Second Coming. Another says the Kingdom of God is now. The first group ignores "dirty politics" and all the running sores of society and "passes by on the other side." The second group gets to be great "armchair revolutionaries," ignoring personal regeneration (the new birth) and ignoring or denying Christ's return. The New Testament says the Kingdom of God is "here now," "is now coming" and "will come."

The church has a greater work than evangelism. In fact, evangelism is only one important part of that work of reconciliation. The church is in the world on His mission—to minister. Evangelism is at the heart

138

of the mission because it begins with man's personal
basic need for new birth. As Christ, the church is
interested in and involved in man's whole life. Whatever God is doing in the reconciliation of man's brokenness and alienation, He is doing it through His church.
This is exactly what He means when He says He is
giving to this church that He has spoken into existence
"the keys to the Kingdom of God" (Matthew 16:19).
Until Christ returns and "the kingdoms of this world
become the kingdoms of our God and His Christ," the
church is working on God's administrative plan for His
world in redemptive acts and reconciling love, incarnating Jesus Christ in the market place, the halls of
justice, the hospitals and mental institutions—wherever
men hurt or are broken or alienated. The church is to
be involved with the world. In that sense it is a
"worldly church."

The third concept of the New Testament regarding
the nature of the new community relates the individual
believer and the local church to the church all over
the world. This conceives of the church as a community of God's people. There is a great need for that
small community of believers to know that they are a
part of the family of God everywhere, who number in
the millions and who are out of every tribe and tongue
and nation. Peter points out the relationship between
the church and the people of God as "a new race" and
"a holy nation" (I Peter 2:9). This church is not hung
up on man's culture because it has a culture all its
own as a "new race of man."

The people of God have a world vision. If the designation "people" relates the church to Christians everywhere, the word "community" relates the church to the
small group who have created a new focus for fellowship in a local place. The focus is life in Jesus Christ
by rebirth. The church does not teach WASP ethics
for it has an ethic all its own, the Sermon on the
Mount. It can be planted in Russia, Germany, Latin

139

America or anywhere and grow and evangelize and minister because ultimately "our citizenship is in heaven, from which also we eagerly wait for a Saviour, the Lord Jesus Christ" (Philippians 3:20 NASB). The church is a local community of believers who are a part of the people of God everywhere. This is the reason a Christian alone is always grateful to discover another Christian.

David Fite, a missionary to Cuba, was imprisoned by the communist government of Cuba. He was given word that he was going to be transferred to the prison camp on the Isle of Pines. He knew that there would be no other Christians there because of a deliberate plan to separate the Christians from one another. Describing his truck ride to the Isle of Pines camp, he tells how depressed and discouraged he became at the prospect of not having a Christian with whom to study the Bible and discuss matters of God. He arrived at the prison camp and was shown his bunk and where to stow his belongings. As he was climbing into his bunk he heard a voice say, "Hermano Daveed?" All of a sudden, he said, there was community, there was the church, for that voice said, "Brother David? Even though there are only two of us, there is the church."

In New Zealand, I had a similar experience. I was traveling with Bruce Stewart, then Director of Evangelism for the New Zealand Baptist Union. We had put the car on the overnight ferry to cross Cook Strait to the South Island. It was early in the morning when we got the car off the ferry and started driving across the South Island to the Tasman Sea. We were far out in the bush when we realized how hungry we were. We came upon a sheep station and went in and asked the man who ran the station if his wife would mind fixing our breakfast, because we were very hungry. He talked to her and she agreed to do it. As it was winter in the Southern Hemisphere, he fixed a small fire in a fireplace against the chill of the July morning. We stood with our backs to the fire, talking. The proprietor worked, sweeping and cleaning and, as we learned, listening. He came to us and said, "I have heard your conversation and it is obvious that you are Christians. Would you mind if my wife came and talked with you while you eat? She is a Christian and it is lonely out here for her. She seldom gets to talk to a Christian." We told him that we would be delighted with her company at breakfast and asked them both to join us.

We sat down to bacon and egg pie and coffee (for the American) and ate and talked about the things of God. All of a sudden, in that remote sheep station, there was community, the church, the family of God. We sensed and felt the presence of the Holy Spirit. When we told our wonderfully hospitable New Zealand friends good-by, the wife said, "You know I feel like I have been to church." And she really had been, for "where two or three Christians are gathered, there am I among them" (Matthew 18:20).

The New Community Is Sharing

To the new community in Corinth, Paul writes, "The grace of the Lord Jesus Christ, and the love of God, and the fellowship of the Holy Spirit be with you all." The believer is "born again of the Spirit" (Gal. 4:29) and called out of the world into the family of God, the new community. The gift of the Holy Spirit to the community of believers is sharing (*koinonia*). This Greek word is usually translated "fellowship" but, in many churches, it has come to mean church suppers, get-togethers, fun and games in the church basement, Coke and hot dogs for the youth. The basic root meaning of *koinonia* is more apt to get to the true nature of the gift of the Holy Spirit to the new community. That

141

basic and root meaning is "sharing." "If we walk in the light as He is in the light, we share with one another, and the blood of Jesus Christ keeps on cleansing us from sin" (I John 1:9).

In giving a person His life, Christ shares with that person all that He is. It is natural, then, that the life of the new community should be one of sharing. Churches are literally packed with hurting and broken people who cry out for help, yet no one hears or cares. One can sit in a church and look through the sea of heads trying to see the religious show going on at the front and never see their faces. People go away as hungry as they came. Someone has said that large churches are churches where no one knows anyone else and they are glad they don't and that small churches are churches where everyone knows everyone else and they are sorry they do! There are churches where this is not so, but, in too many cases, it is true.

Paul writes to the Philippian community of faith about the kind of relationship they are to have with one another. "If therefore there is any encouragement in Christ, if there is any consolation of love, if there is any fellowship of the Spirit, if any affection or compassion, make my joy complete by being of the same mind, maintaining the same love, united in spirit, intent on one purpose. Do nothing from selfishness or empty conceit, but with humility of mind let each of you regard one another as more important than himself; do not merely look out for your own personal interests, but also for the interest of others. Have this attitude in yourselves which was also in Christ Jesus" (Philippians 2:1-5 NASB). It is quite certain that the kind of sharing this passage describes is not what is found in the "knife and fork club" in the average church. There is a deep kind of sharing that comes out of being born of the Spirit. Anything that is done at a church social can probably be done as well or better in some secular organization. There is no real New Testament sharing in the average church because it is not expected, it is not taught, it is not a part of the "program."

The kind of sharing we need in the church is evident in the New Testament. "And they were constantly giving themselves to the apostles' teaching, and to sharing, to the breaking of bread and prayer" (Acts 2:42). In verse 44 of the same chapter it says, "And they began selling their property and possessions, and were sharing them with all, as anyone had need." It was a dangerous time to be a Christian. They were driven from their homes and persecuted. There was a need, so they met the need by sharing all they had and all they were. Is the fellowship of believers in the average church like that in the Book of Acts? And what is even more pressing is the question of what kind of church is needed in the community today to be the sharing community for those who have found new life in Jesus Christ through a new birth?

Is activity the measure of God's community? A full program with something for everyone; the lights on every night; something going on all the time; are these the measure of a church? Is it growth—adding people every Sunday to the membership? Is it buildings bursting at the seams—wall to wall people? Is it crowd-getting religious spectaculars that keep people on a continuous religious high? Is it a highly organized church with all the machinery well oiled and a highly trained staff with well-written job descriptions? A church can have all these things, but, without sharing, it is only doing something that the world can do better. A spiritual sharing community can be well organized, it can be growing, it can be active, but none of these things, singly or collectively, can make a group of people the new community of sharing.

The new community shares its life in Christ. It is not primarily a matter of evangelism, although evangelism is involved. A free translation of Philippians 2:5 used in a previous paragraph is, "Let your attitudes to one another spring out of your new life in Christ." The church is the body of Christ and He is the Head of the body. "For just as we have many members in one body [the human body] and all the members do not have the same function, so we, who are many [the church, the body of Christ], are one body in Christ and each one members one of another" (Romans 12: 4, 5). Christ is the Head of the church (Ephesians 1:22). What is it that gives the human body unity, harmony and correlation? It is the head. The thing that makes the human body more than just a combination of various minerals, elements and water is life. The thing that makes a church the new community, the people of God, and the family of God is life. It is the life of Christ. This life is shared with one another. The church is a spiritual community because it has spiritual life. Those who have life through a new birth are gathered by the Holy Spirit into a community of faith. They are gathered around the person of Christ (Matthew 18:20).

When believers pray, they pray in the name of Jesus Christ. They believe His promise, "And whatever you ask in My Name, that will I do, that the Father may be glorified in the Son" (John 14:13 NASB). The ministry of the Holy Spirit in the church is to constantly remind the church of their source of life and strength. "But the Helper, the Holy Spirit whom the Father will send in My Name, He will teach you all things, and bring to your remembrance all that I said to you" (John 14:26 NASB). Jesus Christ is the glory of God (John 1:14). The Father is always glorified in His Son Jesus Christ (John 17:1-4; John 13:31,32). The life of every believer and the life of the church is life in Christ. Christians share His life in us and admonish each other as we sing the words of Henry Lyle Lambdin:

144

Be thou to Christ, His Body,
Hold fast to Christ Thy Head;
Be thou Christ's open letter
By all men to be read;
Be thou Christ's holy temple,
Himself the corner-stone;
Be thou Christ's living altar
Whereon His love is shown.

Head of the Church inspire us
To have in us Thy mind,
To humbly wait Thy guidance,
Thy joy in serving find.
Bestow the Spirit's grace-gifts
To serve the common good,
While helping each the other
To love Thy brotherhood.

In the new community, people share with one another. In this fellowship every person is free to be his or her true self. In the new birth, one discovers a new beginning of openness and honesty. In Christ, we are born free. God does not kill individuality in the experience of the new birth. Indeed, individuality becomes more meaningful. Believers are individuals unlike the "living dead," the "zombies" of this world who wear a faceless mask of anonymity. We are drawn together at the center to Jesus Christ but left at the circumference with all individual traits. The Christian sees self and others as they really are. The new community rejoices in the different gifts and the different personalities that are represented. There are churches that want to make everyone into the image of what a certain culture sees Christians as being. These churches are usually not open to people who are "different." They have hang-ups about certain life styles or certain races. They are constantly giving out an aura of "they just aren't our kind of people." The new birth gives us common life

145

in Christ, which is the magnet around which we are drawn.

The new community is a community of "saints" (Ephesians 1:1; Philippians 1:1) who also know they are a community of "sinners." They are not afraid to confess sin and failure. The self-righteous man is very uncomfortable in the kind of environment where people speak freely of their weaknesses, their failures and their sin. One does not have to wear the mask of a contrived holiness. In the new community they "confess their sins to one another" (James 5:16). To love and be loved, to forgive and be forgiven are capacities that are given to believers in the new birth. These capacities are brought to the community of faith.

The community is a fellowship of people who have been "surprised by joy." They are delivered from a terrible burden when they no longer have to act out a charade of holiness, but can be their true selves. The community doesn't need a set time to hear confessions. The whole life style and conversation is in the light of the truth that believers are sinners saved by grace and that they qualify for nothing except eternal mercy.

People who are hurt and broken by their sins and their failures may visit a church looking for help and hope but find only a sterile sanctuary. They look at the backs of the people in front of them. They hear a man thunder out against all the sins of man and society. The whole impression is that they have violated the sanctity of the holy place by their presence. There is no saving word that says, "Come, friend, be at peace and at home. You are with sinners just like yourself. We have found something that can help. We have found the everlasting mercy. We have found a life so new that it is called a new birth. It has not made us perfect. We are babes, growing in our new experience of joy. Come, friend, we can help you. Come to the mercy-seat. Know the joy of loving and being loved, the joy of forgiving and being forgiven. We do not have all the answers,

146

but we do have the answer. In this place, those of us who are trying, with His help, to be like Him are gathered. We welcome you."

One problem is evident. Even churches with large numbers of people who have been born again and feel this kind of sharing is needed find it impossible because the structures of the church are not conducive to it. The services are so constructed that the only person who speaks freely is the pastor and he is often chained to delivering a well-prepared sermon that may speak to problems and sins but does not speak to the human heart that hurts and is broken. He does not speak as "the chief of sinners." He often sounds like God's Moses speaking from the burning mountain the "thou shalt nots" of God. The sinner often goes away with a greater load of guilt than when he came. There is no word that "there is a balm in Gilead, there is a physician there." If no one else in the church is sharing the truth that he, too, is a sinner, saved by grace, that man in the pulpit needs to be sharing it.

Small groups in the church such as Sunday school classes, women's groups, men's societies and others could become healing, helping, hopeful sharing groups if they could be freed from studying the lesson, planning for the next meeting, raising money for the new building and a thousand other preoccupations that concern the institution rather than the people. The church needs to discover a new agenda for sharing its common life in Christ in new and exciting ways. It may require a serious overhaul of some of the outdated and fossilized structures. A great computer company, in competing for a contract for creating the "brain" for one of our space flights, tore down all the walls that separated people on the team and created a "community of sharing" which shared failures and successes. They got rid of the walls of the rooms and created one room in which people could move around and talk

147

freely, creating a caring community. They won the contract.

The new community shares its burdens. There are really two kinds of burdens. The first burden that men bear is the troubles that come to all of us. "Man that is born of woman is of few days, and full of trouble" (Job 14:1 AV). It is these burdens of other people that we share. "Bear one another's burdens, and in this way obey the law of Christ" (Galatians 6:2). There are burdens that come, not as a result of sin or failure, but as part of living amid the agony of man's life.

"I haven't heard from Fred in three weeks. He just left. I don't know where he is."

"John found out he has cancer. He won't talk. He won't eat. He just sits and stares. I don't know what to do."

"Amy told me she's pregnant. She is such a good girl. I don't know how this could happen. It's like a nightmare."

Being born again is becoming more aware than ever of the agony and ecstasy of human life. It is coming to know Christ "in the fellowship of His sufferings" (Philippians 3:10). He suffered, the just for the unjust, "that He might bring us to God" (I Peter 3:18). In the church, people share what other people suffer and, by that sharing, we bring them to the healing power of God. People who have the life of Christ in them through the new birth are like him in this way.

There are other kinds of burdens to be borne by ourselves alone and not put on others. "For each one shall bear his own burdens" (Galatians 6:5). Some have said that there is a serious conflict between verse two and verse five of that chapter of Galatians. A careful reading of the text, however, will reveal that, in verse two, Paul is speaking about personal troubles and, in verse five, he is speaking about our work. The new community has work to do and each one must do his fair share of the work and not put it on someone else.

Most of the burden of the work of a church is too often carried by a few and the rest of the people are freeloaders. Jesus said, "We must work the works of Him who sent Me, as long as it is day; night is coming, when no man can work" (John 9:4 NASB). The life of Christ in the believer gives a commitment to the work of Christ. Church leaders complain that they cannot enlist people to do the work of Christ. Can it be that they do not have in them the life of Christ? Asking those who have no new life in Christ to do the work of Christ is like pleading with dead men to fight a battle. In the new community, believers bear one another's troubles and carry their own fair share of the work.

The New Community Is Gifted

Christ gifts His church. He gifts the church by gifting believers. Talents are a consequence of the first physical birth. They are a result of genes that are inherited from our forebears. The spiritual gifts are a consequence of the second birth and are a result of the work of the "Holy Spirit of promise" (Ephesians 1:13). These gifts are given to the believer when he is born again, but each gift needs to be discovered and cultivated. The gifts of the believer are manifestations of the Holy Spirit's work in the believer and are for the common good and not for personal glorification. "But to each one is given the manifestation of the Spirit for the common good. For to one is given the word of wisdom through the Spirit, and to another the word of knowledge according to the same Spirit" (I Corinthians 12:7-8 NASB).

149

There is no evidence that these gifts are given or exercised outside of the common life of God's community of faith. There is no pride in the gift that Christ has given through His Spirit. They are grace-gifts. In two of the three great passages on spiritual gifts they are vitally connected with the word "grace" (Romans 12:3-8; Ephesians 4:7-12). They are not deserved and did not come as a result of some kind of special experience. They were not given because of some special kind of dedication. They are no more of "works" than the experience of salvation.

Let's get it right about spiritual gifts. There are many exciting new experiences in Jesus Christ. But there is no experience "beyond" that experience with Jesus Christ in which we were "born of God." To know Jesus Christ as personal Lord and Savior is to know the Father and to know and be indwelt by the Holy Spirit. There is only one God. If, after you have been born again, you discover your gift and how to use it, remember that the gift was given you when you were born again. There are some people who talk about the discovery of gifts as if they have come into something higher or better than knowing Jesus Christ. When one is born of the Spirit, he or she is "in Christ" and there is no higher position or knowledge than that. "If then you have been raised up [given new life] with Christ, keep on seeking the higher things, where Christ is seated at the right hand of God" (Colossians 3:1). The Holy Spirit is the Spirit of Christ, and Christ is the Son of God. You can grow in your knowledge of Him, but He is all in all. There are people who claim a certain gift and then say that the gift is due to some superior knowledge or surrender that they have attained. This attitude is false and destructive of the community of the faith.

If the three extended passages on spiritual gifts are correlated (Ephesians 4:4-16; I Cor. 12:14; Romans 12:3-8), some conclusions about these gifts that are given to "each one of us" (I Corinthians 12:7) are apparent. First, every believer has been given one or more of the grace-gifts. Second, these gifts are in the New Testament and must be considered seriously. Third, these gifts are gifts of Christ and they must not be confused with our talents. Fourth, the list of gifts is small in number and cannot mean that these are all the gifts that Christ has given. Fifth, in these gifts, the Father has provided for all that the church needs for growth. Sixth, it is the gifts that make the church a body. Seventh, when the members of the body discover and use their gifts, the church grows.

There is a tendency to avoid all teaching concerning spiritual gifts because of fear of some of them. "Healing" and "tongue speaking" are cases in point. Because of this fear, many denominations have become afraid of the great word "charismatic." But the gifts are so much a part of New Testament revelation that they cannot be avoided by anyone who takes the New Testament seriously. Part of the confusion lies in identifying the gifts as specific gifts rather than as classifications of gifts. In Ephesians 4 the gifts are all gifts of Christ to the office bearers of the church to "equip the saints to do the work of ministry" (Ephesians 4:12). He gave gifts to "the sent out ones" (apostles), who were like our missionaries today. He gave some the gift to apply the Word of God to the times in which they lived (prophecy). There are pastors and preachers today who are especially gifted in prophetic preaching (applying the Word of God to the present day). There are those who are gifted in making the gospel understandable to those who have never heard (evangelists). There are those who are gifted as the pastor-teacher of the community of believers. They have a gift for shepherding and feeding the flock of God. But all of these gifted people were given to the church to "equip the saints for the work of ministry." These are gifts given to the office bearers of the church to use in assisting members of the new community to discover

151

and use their gifts in the work of the community, their ministry to one another and their ministry and witness in the world.

There are three other lists of gifts: Romans 12:3-8 list seven gifts; I Corinthians 12:8-10 lists nine gifts; and I Corinthians 12:28-30 lists eight gifts. Again if we correlate the lists some clear classifications are discovered:

1) The gift of preaching (prophecy) is for proclaiming God's revelation of Himself in Jesus Christ.

2) The gift of wisdom is to know the will of God in all matters that concern the church and others.

3) The gift of faith is to channel God's blessings into the lives of others.

4) The gift of teaching is to make plain the Word of God and the claims that it makes on us.

5) The gift of "knowledge speaking" is to make eternal truth plain and to apply it to everyday life.

6) The gifts of the Holy Spirit (mercy and lovingkindness) are to make the love of God and the compassion of Jesus Christ flow into the lives of other people.

7) The gift of discernment of spirits is to make clear the purity of our motives.

8) The gift of administration (government) is to keep order (organization) in the life and work of the church.

9) The gift of "useful helps" is for ministries to the church and to the world.

10) The gift of healing is for special ministries to the sick, the broken and the hurting in the church and in the world.

11) Special gifts of "miracles" are for special signs of God's presence and power.

Because so many who are born again become caught up in, and many times become confused by, the matter of "tongue speaking," an additional word is needed on this subject. Tongue speaking is not mentioned in the passage in Romans, but occurs last in both lists in I Corinthians 12. The Corinthian church delighted in the gift of tongues. Because there were so many excesses, Paul takes up three chapters (12, 13 and 14) in his first letter to this church to discuss the matter of tongue speaking. To help control it, he gives the church some guidelines. He says, "I have given you a list of gifts; desire the greater gifts, not the lesser ones" (12:13). In the list given, tongue speaking is last. He tells them he once spoke in tongues as an immature Christian but, when he became mature, he gave it up. "When I was a child, I babbled like a child but when I became a man I put away childish things" (13:11).

The thirteenth chapter is about gifts. He says that no gift is as important as love (13:13). Paul wants the Corinthians to speak for God in a language everyone can understand (14:2-3). Tongue speaking may build up the one who speaks, but one who speaks words of comfort, exhortation and truth to the church will be much more helpful to the whole church (14:1-4). Tongue speaking is like a lack of harmony in music (14:7). Tongue speaking makes us sound like barbarians to those who do not understand (14:11). He says, in verse twelve, to the Corinthians, who love this gift so much, "Because you are so eager for spiritual things, why don't you pay attention to the gifts that build the church?" Paul would rather speak five words that people can understand than ten thousand words in tongues (14:19). He calls them to maturity, to come out of their "baby ways" (14:20). The Corinthian community of believers was beset by serious problems with immature Christians who thought the world began and ended with tongue speaking. It is interesting to note that they were the church that was last and least in their giving to a needy world (II Corinthians 8,9).

The gifts, as they are discovered and used, are what makes the church a body. This is the whole thrust of the analogy of the human body in Romans 12. The body

153

is a unity because of the head. If the different organs and members of the body fail to function, the whole body is affected. The less dramatic gifts are more important than the dramatic and they are always listed first. The church can go for a long time without a miracle, but it needs the gift of "useful helps" every day. Healing the brokenness of a divorcee is just as much healing as a complete remission of cancer. In most churches, everyone comes to hear one man demonstrate his gift of preaching, while all the others "sit on" their gift.

Tom Henderson was a steel mill man. A week after Tom was born again, he came into the church study and stood before me and said, "Brother John, you know I never got past the fourth grade. I think God wants me to witness to people in the hospital. When I visit in the hospital, I just feel I've got to help."

I had laid on the hearts of the people the need for a hospital ministry of compassion and healing. We were getting hundreds of calls each week from shut-in people and people in the hospital as a result of a radio program. Tom was answering my call. God gave Tom the gift of compassion and healing. He had the gift from the moment of his new birth. He led many other people to an experience of new birth in Christ. In two years, nurses and Roman Catholic sisters were calling us and requesting "Reverend Henderson" to come and make a call. He was no "reverend." He was a steel mill man with a fourth grade education. Christ gifted him at his second birth with the gift of compassion and healing.

More than twenty years have gone by. Recently, I was in the city where I was then pastor and I saw Tom in the congregation. After the service, he came to me and hugged me and said, "Brother John, I'm still doing it. I was in the hospitals this afternoon and God gave me the most wonderful experience. . . ." He found his

154

gift and he was using that gift in ministry. Only eternity will reveal how effective he is as a witness. Tom did not "sit on" his gift.

One should know that the exercise of our gift in loving, Christlike ministry is not "cheap grace." It is linked with crucifixion. "The Son of Man did not come to be ministered to, but to minister and give his life a purchase price for many" (Matthew 20:28). When one begins to follow in the footsteps of Christ to begin a ministry, somewhere down that road there will be a cross. No one ever decides to serve others without the crucifixion of self. The rhythm of His life was incarnation, crucifixion, resurrection. To follow Him may mean a cross, but on the other side of the skull-shaped hill is an empty tomb. At the time of our new birth, as part of our spiritual heritage, we are endowed with one or more gifts that we are to use for the glory of God, the building up of the church-body, and our witness ministry to the world. When these gifts are exercised within the discipline of the church, under the leadership of the Spirit and the headship of Christ, they will lead us to making the Word flesh, to the crucifixion of self, to His final "well done."

The local church is the family of God gathered in a community, a part of God's people ministering to themselves and to the world as they exercise their gifts. The one way into this living organism is by new birth. This new social order, the new community of God's people, seeks to live by dying. It never creates social barriers but crosses them. It never causes suffering but ministers to suffering. It bears no weapons but love. It loves all things, believes all things, bears all things. It suffers long but is kind. It has only one object and one goal—to share His love with the whole world. This is what our Lord expects of His community.

The church is not always what it needs to be. One needs to consider that the church is a supernatural

155

body and a human community at one and the same time. Like every member of the body, the church itself is caught in the tension between what it is and what it ought to be. The church, like the new believer, is in a growing experience to maturity.

The sad thing is that some churches have not faced the challenge to become a living, growing community of the reborn. No one is capable of being a judge as to whether or not a given church is really the body of Christ or just another institution interested only in its own survival. That is the responsibility of the Lord of the Harvest. But one thing is certain, that Christ has given the commission to the church, the new community. The church will have to answer to the Householder when He returns and asks each church for an accounting of its stewardship (Matthew 24:44-51). Who will answer for grace-gifts unrecognized and uncultivated? Who will answer for sermons that did not make clear, "You must be born again?" Who will answer for persons who died, unloved and unloving, in the shadow of our churches without a loving word from us?

Imagine how "An Open Letter to the Church from the World" might read:

Dear Church:

What we want from you, church, is only one thing—be the good news. Don't tell us about a Christ who died two thousand years ago. Show us a living Christ in your own personal lives. We want no words from you except those red with the blood of your sacrifice, not His. We don't want the word, but the Word made flesh.

Never ask us to be gripped by our emotions when you talk to us about a Savior on the cross, unless you are gripped by your own emotions. Don't try to prove anything to us, because for every doubt you

156

settle you raise one hundred more that you can't settle. Don't give us facts about Christ—we can read as well as you—tell us what He has done in your life.

If you preach to us, look at your sermon and cut out all the high-sounding phrases—we get enough of those from the politicians. Cut out everything your church expects you to say and just give us what you have to say so badly it hurts. Above all, please do not beat us with words. We know how bad we are. Just show us people who are in the grip of something from the Beyond, something real and powerful. Then we will repent, believe and be reborn.

Don't try to entertain us. Hot chocolate and cookies in the church basement cannot compete with TV and nightclubs for entertainment. If you want to show us something, tear off your mask and show us the glory of God in the face of a sinner saved by grace. Don't give us little things that the world can give better. We want to know about life, love, death, heaven and hell. If you have some answers, share them with us.

Help us build a better world. There are poor, hungry people. There are slums not fit for pigs, let alone people. I'm afraid to walk on the streets at night. My kids are experimenting with drugs. Don't give me lectures on these subjects; I can get those on TV. If your Christ is the answer for these problems, don't tell me about it—show me. Where were your people when that low-income housing project had a disaster last year and we were trying to move twenty thousand people in the dead of winter to new housing? If you were in your easy chairs watching it on TV, don't talk to me about love!

By the way, church, if I happen to get my life straight, and become a member, don't stick a package of offering envelopes in my hand right off the bat. Teach me that there are things more important than money.

157

If you really want me to become a Christian, don't tell me about the sterile nursery for my baby. Don't show me the crystal chandelier that cost twenty-five thousand dollars. Don't tell me about the four degrees that your pastor holds. Tell me about the lives that have been changed by your ministries. Show me the grace-gifts that adorn the lives of your people. Tell me about the kids that have new daddies, the wives that have new husbands, the cities that have new citizens because you were "salt" and "light" and "leaven" for a mad, mad world.

Don't kid me about yourself, church. I can read the newspapers. I know about your members in high places, who sold themselves for gold or glory or greed. Don't tell me that the church is for good people. Tell me it is for sinners. Tell me that well people don't need a doctor; only the sick need one. Tell me that new life in Christ is a whole lifetime and that I begin with a new birth. Tell me that nobody's perfect. Tell me I can be better than I am. Better than that, *show* me how I can be better.

One last word, church. Don't tell me how much Jesus loves me. Tell me if you love me. Show me your tears for my heartache. Show me your searchings for my lostness. Show me that you care about this ache in my gut and this sob in my throat and this knife in my conscience when I am all alone.

I guess I'm kind of like the preachers. I said that was my last word, but I want to lay another one on you before I close. You know that guy you sent to see me last week? Don't send him back. All he talked about was hell. Man, I need a talk on how hot hell is like I need a hole in the head. Do I know about hell? I'm living in it. Marge said she's going to leave me. I don't know where one of my kids is right now— she ran away. The boy is nothing but trouble. Hey, if you've got somebody that can help me with the hell I'm in right now, send them around. If you've got somebody who knows what it's like to live in hell, who's got it all together now, who's got answers, not sermons, send him.

Yours sincerely,
THE WORLD

P.S. Hey, I forgot—you know I asked you to send somebody to see me. Tell him to come on **Wednesday** night. Wednesday is a lousy night for TV.

How can I forget her? She walked into that mission last night like a zombie. Seventeen years old, pregnant, mainlining. I went with students from the seminary to the mission they had started right in the middle of hell in the Vieux Carré, across the street from the homosexual bar. At the door was a student greeting those who came in, "Good evening, friend, God loves you."

She walked right by him, her dilated pupils staring straight ahead—walked stiff-legged, as a pregnant woman does. She was almost across the room. She stopped, trying to think in the blurred fuzziness of the drug, "What did he say?" She came back, as if sleepwalking. "What did you say?"

The young man said, "I said, 'Good evening, God loves you.' "

She said, "Hell man, there ain't no such thing as love. If there is, nobody loves me."

How could I tell her about God's love? I tried. How do you get through to a drugged mind? I told her that I loved her and she giggled, as if I were talking about sex. I was teaching evangelism in a seminary and couldn't get through to a poor little girl who was living in hell. How do you tell people about a love relationship in which people really care because God cares about them? How do you tell them, when they have lost all ability to understand? The meanings that words had for her were not the same as for me. I wonder if anyone ever really loved that girl? I know God does. How could I tell her? She needs a new birth of love.

7.

A NEW BIRTH OF LOVE

"And this is the message we have heard from Him and announce to you, that God is light, and in Him there is no darkness at all. If we say that we have fellowship with Him and yet walk in the darkness we lie and do not practice the truth" (I John 1:5,6).

"Beloved, let us love one another, for love is from God; and everyone who loves is born of God and knows God. The one who does not love does not know God, for God is love. By this the love of God was manifested in us, that God has sent His only begotten Son into the world so that we might live through Him. . . . By this we know that we abide in Him and He in us, because He has given us of His Spirit. And we have beheld and bear witness that the Father has sent the Son to be the Savior of the world. Whoever confesses that Jesus is the Son of God, God abides in him, and he in God. And we have come to know and have believed the love which God has for us. God is love, and the one who abides in love abides in God, and God abides in him. By this, love is perfected with us, that we may have confidence in the day of judgment; because as He is, so also are we in this world. There is no fear in love; but perfect love casts out fear because fear involves punishment, and the one who fears is not perfected in love. We love, because He first loved us" (I John 4:7-9, 13-19).

"Whoever believes that Jesus is the Christ is born of God; and whoever loves the Father loves the child born of Him. By this we know that we love the children of God when we love God and observe His commandments. For this is the love of God, that we keep His commandments; and His commandments are not burdensome. For whatever is born of God overcomes the world; and this is the victory that has overcome the world—our faith" (I John 5:1-4).

It is not easy to sing about love in our world. Young people sing, "Love makes the world go round," and, "What the world needs is love sweet love" and, "Love is a many splendored thing." Where is love in the agony of Northern Ireland or in the continuing Arab-Israeli conflict? Where is love in terrorists holding children captive while they bargain for their "rights"? Where is love when one out of every three marriages is dissolved? Where is love when a battered child is brought to a hospital broken both physically and spiritually? Where is love when corporations cheat the public in their greed? Where is love when the earth is raped and its streams and atmosphere polluted for the "quick buck"? It is not very difficult to believe what Arthur Guiterman suggested:

> *"Where did you come from?"*
> *The pilgrim answered, "Earth,*
> *A fevered planet but I loved it well."*
> *Around him rang in soft celestial mirth,*
> *"Why, that was Hell."*

We are living in a violent society. The handgun is the cause of many of the murders committed in my

162

Atlanta, as elsewhere. It is difficult to get any kind of handgun legislation because of misguided patriots who confuse the Revolutionary War militia with the private citizen of today. The sale of handguns is big business and its powerful lobby is difficult to overcome.

Our education in violence begins at an early age, on television and in the theater. Spectacles in group brutality are arranged for us in professional football. All that is violent and destructive in man is highlighted on the news media. It is like hell, as in John Milton's *Paradise Lost:*

> Blood trod upon the heels of blood;
> Revenge in desperate mood, at midnight met
> Revenge; war brayed back to war; deceit deceived
> Deceit, lie cheated lie, and treachery
> Mined under treachery, and perjury
> Swore back to perjury and blasphemy, and curse
> Loud answered curse; and drunkard stumbling fell
> O'er drunkard fallen; and husband, husband met
> Returning each from other's bed defiled;
> Thief stole from thief, and robber on the way
> Knocked robber down; and lewdness, violence
> And hate met lewdness, violence and hate.
> And mercy, weary with beseeching, had
> Retired behind the sword of Justice, red
> With ultimate and unrepenting wrath.

Life, Light and Love

In the first two chapters of John's first epistle he tells us that God is light. Light in this instance means more than the fact that God has revealed Himself. It is moral light. John's gospel is the gospel of conflict between light and darkness. He opens his gospel with "and the light shined in the darkness and the darkness could not put it out" (John 1:5). The struggle is a suspense thriller comparable to J.R.R. Tolkien's *Lord of the Rings*. Hitler could burn thousands of Jews in his ovens, but he could not put out the light. Herod could kill children by the thousands, but he could not put out the light. The Soviets can stretch their Gulag Archipelago over one-third of the world, but they cannot put out the light. No combination of men on earth and demons in hell can put out the light.

God is light in man's moral darkness. The light that is God helped Moses to come down from the burning mountain with the Ten Commandments. The light that is God helped expose the corruption of Watergate. When evil becomes so entrenched, so overbearing, so authoritarian, then the light shines in the darkness. The dark hours of man's history have always been the hours of apocalypse—revelation of the light. Even the nations that did not have the Mosaic law had the light. "For when the Gentiles who do not have the law do by instinct what the law says is right, these who do not have a law are a law for themselves in that they show that the law is written in their conscience which bears witness to them saying that something is right or wrong" (Romans 2:14,15). It is for this reason that God will judge all men—because they have all had the light.

The light has more significance for man living in the moral darkness of his own creation. Man's problem is an identity problem. He does not know who he is. God as light is a revelation that man is the creation of God. "There was the true light which came into the world and gives light to every man. He was in the world—the world that He made—and the world did not recognize Him" (John 1:9-10). Because man does not know who he is, he behaves like the accident of evolution he believes himself to be. When he murders, rapes, steals, hates and fornicates, he is the "naked ape" reverting to the jungle. His bestiality and inhumanity are all explained as reversions to primitive urges that a few more centuries or millenniums of evolution hopefully will cure. The authors of our Declaration of Independence knew that if man's life, liberty and pursuit of happiness were to endure they must be endowments of the Creator and not accidents of history. The "fall" of man is his no longer knowing that He is the creation of God. Hell is not knowing who you are. We are living in a hell on earth because men no longer know who they are. When men live in the light of God and know that they are His by creation, they have self-respect, dignity and right relationships with their fellows. There is no essential difference between a domestic altercation that leads to a shooting and a war declared or undeclared between peoples. It is not hard to kill men as long as they are "ginks," or "gooks" or "Japs" or "honkies" or "niggers." When we see a man as God's creation and he is depraved, we are depraved. When one is deprived, we are deprived. We are the ones "for whom the bell tolls" because "no man is an island."

God is light in His self-revelation. He reveals man as the creation of God. God is love (I John 4:8). Love is the very nature of God. God as love is a revelation of God's attitude toward us in our sin and rebellion. If God were only light, we couldn't stand to be near Him. The light of His holiness would be too much for us. He is love, and His love was made clear by His sending His Son into the world (I John 4:9). If God were light only, and we knew we were sinners, we would be afraid to approach Him. But John says, "In love there is no fear, for perfect love eliminates fear" (I John 4:18). Love even takes away the fear of God's judgment for sin (I John 4:17). Because God is love, we can approach Him without fear.

Jesus Christ came into the world to show us what

God is like and called God "Father." The fact that God is love has another side. "Beloved, if God loved us in this way, we should love one another" (I John 4:11). The answer to man's brutality and violence is love. Man's inhumanity to man is impossible if we love one another. Here is the way to end all war, bloodshed, hatred and animosity. Here is the way to beat the swords into ploughshares and the spears into pruninghooks. Here is the way to get rid of all the handguns. Here is the way to stop all the shootings and stabbings and muggings. It is the way of love. To love God and your neighbor as yourself is the sum total of human goodness.

That sounds very good, doesn't it? Then why isn't it a reality? It all seems very simple. Let's just start loving one another. Let's live up to the light that God has given us. But, you see, it is not enough just to have the light. We have the light and write laws concerning rape and murder, but people still commit rape and murder. We have laws concerning violence, but men are still violent. We know about love, but we hurt most those we love. Why don't we live up to the light we have? Why don't we love people? Religion isn't the answer, not even Christianity. Most of the participants in the Watergate scandal were church members of one denomination or another. Men who wage war with other men are church members. We even have before us the spectacle of Protestant-Catholic war in Northern Ireland. It is not enough to have some of the light or to know about love or even to be religious.

The key is found in the other concept in the first epistle of John. God is life. "What was from the beginning, what we heard, what we saw with our eyes, what our hands touched concerning the Word of Life—and the life was manifested—we saw and bear testimony to you the eternal life which is from the Father and revealed to us" (I John 1:1-2). John's gospel has more testimony. "In Him was life, and the life was the light of men" (John 1:4). Men cannot live up to the light that they have from God and they cannot know and practice real love because they do not have life. They live physically, but they are dead spiritually. What men need is life, life from God, eternal life.

Speaking to the Ephesian Christians who were born again, Paul says, "And you were dead [before your new birth] in your sins and trespasses, which you formerly practiced as is the custom in the world" (Ephesians 2:1,2). He says to the Colossian believers, "And when you were dead in your sins and living in carnality, He made you alive together with Him, having forgiven all your sins" (Colossians 2:13). John relates the whole matter of light and love and life to the new birth. "Beloved, let us love each other, for love is from God; and everyone who loves is born of God and knows God" (I John 4:7). Knowing and loving God are both related to experiential faith and the new birth. Just being religious or accepting the Christian ethic is not enough to change the hearts and actions of men. The moral law, religion, or even knowing about love is not humanity's need. We have all that. We need life. Birth is the way into life. There is no life without birth. *You must be born again.*

Man has to be radically changed at the core of his being. He is a sinner by nature, by choice and by practice, and no amount of moral light or preachments of loving one another will change him. Isaiah, the prophet, saw his nation as a people who had abandoned God:

> Listen, O heavens, and hear O earth;
> For the Lord speaks,
> "Sons I have reared and brought up,
> But they have revolted against Me.
> An ox knows its owner,

And a donkey its master's manger,
But Israel does not know,
My people do not understand.

Alas, sinful nation,
People weighed down with iniquity,
Offspring of evildoers,
Sons who act corruptly!
They have abandoned the Lord,
They have despised the Holy One of Israel,
They have turned away from Him.
Where will you be stricken again,
As you continue in your rebellion?
The whole head is sick,
And the whole heart is faint.
From the sole of the foot even to the head
There is nothing sound in it.
Only bruises, welts, and raw wounds,
Not pressed out or bandaged,
Nor softened with oil.

(Isaiah 1:2-6 NASB)

There is no single shred of evidence in all the history
of mankind that man is becoming better. In spite of all
the talk about evolution into something better, humanism is a bankrupt philosophy. In the theological
liberalism of the 1920s and 1930s there was a great
deal of hope that love would finally conquer and the
spark of divinity in man would be fanned into the flame
of a new kind of man. The Atlanta *Constitution* carried
a headline proclaiming the advent of the millennium at
the close of the First World War. A great Southern
preacher, who really believed that that war was "the
war to end all wars," had a broken heart when the
Second World War became a fact of history. These
misguided hopes of man's divinity were exploded by
man's brutality. Is there any evidence that we are

morally or socially better than people were in the Middle Ages? What about the ancient Chinese civilization? Is ours better than theirs? Is humanity making any progress? Is even our pornography any better than that of ancient Rome? The humanist says, "Look at our hospitals, our orphanages, our social programs on behalf of the poor." Does it make much difference that a person was born in a sterile nursery if you fry him in an electric chair twenty-six years later? Right now we are probably experiencing the greatest famine in world history. At the same time, our modern ingenuity has produced food surpluses. We can visit the moon and Mars and dream of interstellar travel, but we can't provide decent housing for thousands of our citizens. We are sinners both personally and socially.

The radical change that the sin of man demands is a new birth of love. The new birth brings the light and life of God into our lives. Man has a serious case of photophobia. He is afraid of the light. "For every one practicing evil hates the light, and does not come to the light, for fear of exposing his sins. But the one practicing truth comes to the light, that his deeds may be seen as having been done in the sight of God" (John 3:20,21). People who have photophobia dislike talking about God or discussing personal salvation. They may even dislike the experience of hearing any proclamation of the gospel that is probing. We have a master of ceremonies for a radio talk show in Atlanta who becomes very angry when a caller quotes the Scriptures. His poorly disguised irritation is a revealing symptom of photophobia.

In the new birth, we come into possession of the life of God. When we have new life in Christ we are no longer afraid of the light. "Do not participate in their sin for you were formerly in darkness [literally, "you were darkness"], but now you are in light in the Lord; walk as children of light (for the fruit of light is goodness, righteousness and truth)" (Ephesians 5:7-9). The result of the new birth is a new life style of light—walking in it, loving it. One cannot separate the new birth from a moral and ethical revolution. It really involves a new morality. This new morality is not Joseph Fletcher's *Moral Responsibility* or "situation ethics," but *The Sermon on the Mount*, by Jesus Christ.

The Greatest of These Is Love

In knowing God as life, we are born again. Then we know who we are. We know that we are the children of God by faith. This solves our identity crisis. We are no longer lost in a cemetery of dead values. We are not accidents of evolution, the result of blind chance. We are the sons of God. "The ones who are being led by the Spirit of God—these are the sons of God" (Romans 8:14). In knowing God as light we know what is right and what is wrong. We know the difference between the works of the flesh and the fruits of the Spirit. "Now the deeds of the flesh are apparent, which are: immorality, filthiness, indecency, idolatry, witchcraft, animosity, strife, jealousy, temper, anger, envy, drunkenness, wild parties and other things like these about which I have warned you. Those who practice these things will not inherit the Kingdom of God. The fruit of the Spirit is love, joy, peace, patience, kindness, goodness, faithfulness, humility and self-control; against such things there is no law" (Galatians 5:19-23). In knowing God as love, we have the power to live the life of God and to practice the light of God. Love is the "force field'" that keeps us in the life and light of God. What is love? It is not easy to define. As Beilby Porteus wrote:

Love is something so divine,
Description would but make it less;
'Tis what I feel, but can't define.
'Tis what I know, but can't express.

It is very difficult to define love because of the poverty of the English language. Greek (the language in which our New Testament was written) had many words that we would translate as "love" in modern English. The word *epithymia* expressed the need for sensual fulfillment, such as the need for food or sex. The word *eros* expressed the need for aesthetic fulfillment, as in the search for beauty and truth in nature and culture such as in music, arts and philosophy. The word *philia* expressed the need for personal fulfillment in friendship; it also implied the rejection of those who were not friends. The word *agape,* which is God's kind of love, has been neglected, not because *agape* is the greatest kind of love, but because it is love coming into "love" from another direction. It is love coming from God.

The new birth is a "birth from above." The new birth is a discovery of *agape.* We are no longer slaves to our desires. We are in control, because He is in control. The new birth brings a new dimension into our lives, the dimension of eternity. We now know the difference between animal pleasure and rejoicing in God's gift of sex. We now know the difference between getting lost in our search for beauty and the beauty of God's holiness. We now know the difference between loving our friends and hating our enemies, and loving everyone. Our eyes have been opened to see all of God's great and good world and its beauties, and we have the desire to redeem and reconcile where it has been marred and scarred by man's greed and violence. Our remaining problem is getting on with God's purposes in spite of the pull from below that is still with

171

us. Our whole life is (as is the history of mankind) divided into "before Christ" and "after Christ." He is life, light and love in our lives since our "birth from above."

Love Is Concern

We have said that, in the new birth, we discover ultimate reality, ultimate being, God. God has revealed Himself as Father, Son and Holy Spirit—a community of love. In the theology of Paul Tillich, God is the subject of ultimate concern. Man's ultimate concern is God. I am now saying that God is ultimate concern. That man is the subject of God's concern. To put it simply, God cares. Any concern that we may have to know Him comes from Him, from His caring love.

God's revelation of Himself in the Bible and in Jesus Christ came out of His concern. He wants us to know who He is and in what way He loves and cares for us. This concept of God as concern is very different from ideas about God that are apparent in some of the world religions. In Stoicism (as in all Oriental mysticism, including Transcendental Meditation) God is apathy, far above it all, removed and unmoving. By practicing meditation, one could identify with the transcendental God far above the agony and ecstasy of man's life. Some teachers of Stoicism even gave students exercises in not caring. In contrast to this, the God of Abraham, Isaac, Jacob, and Father of our Lord Jesus Christ revealed Himself as being concerned about Israel, the world and the believer. To say that God loves is to say that God is concerned. To say that God is love, is to say that God is concern. We become caring persons because we have a living relationship with the God who is concern.

"If you really cared about me, you would understand me better." Has a child ever said this to a parent? Yes, millions of times since Adam. We link concern and understanding in human relationships. The youth may want a car or a bicycle and we say, "You can't have a car" or "You can't have a bicvcle." We did not take the time to find out why the child wanted the car or the bicycle. The child then feels justly that we did not understand.

When we know God as ultimate concern, we know that He understands us. Jesus talks about the "things" of life—food, drink, clothing and shelter—and says, "Your Father knows that you have need of these things" (Matthew 6:32). He says to us, "Do not be anxious about these things." He really understands the anxieties of life.

You may say to a church visitor, "I don't have time for church and God. I've got to earn a living." Now, you are talking as if He does not know that you have need of the things that honest employment can give you. These are not ultimate concerns, but He knows that they are important. He also knows there are ultimate concerns, that man does not live by bread alone. He is saying to us, "I know that you need to work for a living, and I want to help you with that, but there is something more important—seek first the Kingdom of God."

When we talk about God's really knowing us in our need, we cannot forget that God came in the flesh and lived among us. Ultimate concern became flesh and blood in Jesus of Nazareth. He came to know us as most men are—poor, hungry and dispossessed. He alone, of all men, picked his own parents and he did not opt for a home in the house of a merchant prince or the religious upper middle class or the ruling nobility. He picked for His parents two poor people in the little village of Nazareth. When He came of age, they could not offer two male goats for a sacrifice, but

173

offered two turtle doves, the offering of the poor. He knew the cold dampness of the fisherman's boat and the hard labor of the carpenter's shop. He knew the pain and agony of death in the house of Mary and Martha. He knew raw aching loneliness, praying alone on a mountainside. Yes, He knows we "have need of these things."

He needed a place to sleep many nights. He needed food many days. He needed a cup of cold water during many weary marches on many dusty roads. He knows what it means "to have need of these things." He understood the woman's need for sex at the well of Sychar. He was not shocked by what He already knew, as God —that she sold herself for money. He understood that she was alone and had to live. At the same time, He reminded her of the ultimate concern, water which, after one drink, would release her from her bondage.

Dear one, He understands you. You do not need to tell Him how bad you are. He knows. There is no need to tell Him how good you are, for He knows better.

Another result of knowing God as ultimate concern is a sense of belonging. The new birth experience is an experience of refathering. The major cause of failure in education, industry, finance, and the home is the failure of some people to achieve an identity and a sense of self-worth. Love and self-worth are all mixed up. The child who has not been taught, by fondling and affection, how to love and be loved will be an insecure child and an insecure adult. For some of these people the new birth works a radical transformation. They discover love and, because they now have identity, their whole personality is radically changed.

We need to know that we are a person distinct from all other persons and that the person we are is nice to know. The failure to give and receive love and to attain a sense of self-worth are really the two basic failures of human existence. A teen-age girl, whom I was counseling, expressed to me her need for belonging. She felt that each of her divorced parents only wanted her in order to get even with the other. She had no brothers and sisters and felt that she just didn't belong to anyone who really cared for her as a person. I asked her, "How would you like to have a father who really loved you, an older brother who would be willing to die for you, and as many brothers and sisters who really cared about you as you want?"

She answered quickly and eagerly, "I would like that."

Then I told her about God's love, about Christ, who is not ashamed to call us "family," and about the fellowship of caring Christians. Seeing that she was disappointed, I asked, "What's wrong?"

She said, "I thought you would tell me about someone who is real, that you can see and hug and feel."

I talked with her for some time and finally she agreed to open her heart and her life to Jesus Christ. She committed herself to Christ and she became a part of the fellowship in which I was serving as pastor. A few weeks later, she came into my study one Sunday morning and said, "Brother John, you were right. The Father's real. Jesus is real. And I love my brothers and sisters." She belonged. She found out who she was and how to love and be loved. For her it was life out of death.

One of the keys to the three parables of "lostness" in Luke 15 is that the concern of the woman, the shepherd and the father arose out of the worth that they placed upon the object that was lost. God, in His concern, has placed a value upon us. People matter to God. This worth that God sees in us is not of our own making. "Now remember what you were, my brothers, when God called you. From the human point of view few of you were wise or powerful or of high social standing. . . . Whoever wants to boast must boast of what the Lord has done" (I Corinthians 1:26,31 TEV).

Only as men have worth and dignity before God, are they free.

The degrading thing about slavery was the worth that it put upon humanity. It degraded the slave owner even more than the slave. The present search for roots and the need for man to know who he is and to feel a sense of worth is a search for identity. The greatest discovery one can make is to know that he is infinitely worthwhile to God and that God is ready to give His name by birth and by adoption. The Christian places his value judgment on his brother man out of the gospel and not out of a textbook on sociology.

We could have expected holiness, righteousness and power from God, but He wants us to see His concern. In the blood that ran first red and then black down the wood of the cross, God said how concerned He is. In seven agonizing cries from the cross, the Savior said how much God is concerned. In the gentle, still, small voice of the Spirit's work of conviction, God is saying to us how much He is concerned. He might have sent ten thousand angels armed with missiles to destroy ten cities, so the rest of us would repent. He might have sent a plague that would leave a black death on every corpse, spelling out, "God is not mocked." But because He is Love, ultimate concern, He sent His suffering Servant, who came and, by dying, conquered death, hell and the grave. "And the Lord laid on Him the iniquity of us all" (Isaiah 53:6).

Someone had to go down in the darkness of man's treachery and rebellion. Jesus Christ, the Son, said, "I will go. I came to do your will, O God. I will go" (Hebrews 10:7,9). In Him, God is light—light that shines in the darkness and the darkness cannot put it out. Someone had to go down into man's death and be life—in Him was life, and the life was the light of men. Someone had to go down into man's violent and savage world and be love—and, in Him, God is love, ultimate concern. The value that man has in the sight of God can only be measured by the cross.

Concern gives things meaning. The new birth that brings us into the life of God brings meaning into our lives. There is a purpose behind it all. Man's life means very little unless there is some kind of purpose for his existence. The three basic loves now motivate our whole existence and give it meaning. There is more to sex than physical pleasure. There is more to beauty than a drop of dew upon a rose petal. There is more to friendship than "you only go around once in life."

Sex is giving ourselves to another whom we love, cherish, honor and respect—giving ourselves in such a way that we belong to each other, we are one flesh. Our search for beauty in nature is the pure joy of seeing His fingerprints in budding flowers and hearing His voice in the singing birds, the whisper of the wind and the babbling of the stream. Our friendships are now only a reflection of our ability to love and communicate with Him.

It is a beautiful morning and it is a beautiful day, but, contrary to the lyrics of *Oklahoma,* not "because everything is going my way." It is because He loves me, is concerned about me. He has given me new life in Jesus Christ and meaning to my life. We don't have all the answers for all the questions, but we do have answers for the important ones. We know who we are, why we are here and where we are going.

There is one more word before we leave the matter of God as ultimate concern. God must also be the subject of your ultimate concern. You cannot have life without God. You exist but you do not live without Him. The Bible, the Holy Spirit and the Christian witness lead us into the presence of the One who is ultimate concern. He calls for a living response from you. The Bible says that God is a seeking God and that the initiative is with Him. "We love Him because He first loved us" (I John 4:19). The Bible also says that we need to seek

177

God. "Seek Him with your heart" (Deuteronomy 4:29). "If you seek Him, He will be found" (I Chronicles 28:9). "Early will I seek You" (Psalms 63:1). "You shall seek Me, and you shall find Me" (Jeremiah 29:13). "Seek you the Lord" (Zephaniah 2:3). "Seek you first the Kingdom of God" (Matthew 6:33). "Seek the Lord while He may be found, call upon Him for He is near" (Isaiah 55:6).

He is concerned about you. Are you concerned about knowing Him? Miss Him and you miss everything—life, light and love. God wants you to know who you are by finding out who He is. You are anxious about many things. Are you anxious about your relationship to the living God?

Love Is Commitment

We are familiar with the word commitment in regard to love in the traditional marriage ceremony. It is also a familiar word to those of us who are evangelists of the good news. God requires a commitment from us of the most radical nature. Again, however, we are thinking of God and not man.

Has God committed Himself to us? "But we should always give thanks to God for you, brothers beloved of the Lord, because God has chosen you from the beginning for salvation through sanctification by the Spirit and faith in the truth" (II Thessalonians 2:13). "For whom He foreknew, He also predestined to become conformed to the image of His Son that He might be the first-born among many brothers; and whom He predestined, these He also called; and whom He called, these He made right with God; and whom He made right with God, He also glorified" (Romans 8:29-30). God is committed to us from before the world began. He is committed to our glorification at our Lord's Second Coming. Because He is God, He never changes His mind about His choice. This commitment involves us in the agony and ecstasy of loving. It involves both joy and pain. If you do not want pain, commit yourself to no person. Commit yourself to stamp collections, your work, your career, anything but a person. But we must remind you that the lack of commitment is hell. God is love. Love is commitment. God is committed to us.

Commitment involves a choice. "Just as He chose us in Him before the foundations of the world, that we should be holy and blameless . . . in love" (Ephesians 1:4 NASB). Literally, this verse translates, "Just as He picked us out." Who picked out whom? Did God make a decision to save us by a new birth or did we decide for God and then, because of our decision, God "birthed" us?

Our only daughter is adopted and we always told her she was adopted. We tried to prepare her for meeting other children who might tease her by telling her she was not our "real" girl. We told her how we went to the Missouri Baptist Children's Home and "picked her out." We said, "Now, when the children tease you about being adopted, you tell them that we picked you out of a whole group of children, but their parents had to take what they got.

One day, while I was working on a mower in the back yard, I heard her tell some children about her adoption experience, which she could not have remembered. She said, "I was in the Children's Home and one day a nice-looking man and woman came to the home and the minute I saw them I knew that I wanted them to be my Mother and Daddy. So I went to the woman and told her, 'I want you to be my parents.' She said it was all right and they took me home." Now who picked out whom? In her childlike love she wanted to be the "picker" and make us the "picked." But, really, we

179

did the picking out and she could do nothing to influence the choice.

In our childlike immaturity as born again believers, we feel that we made the choice. It was our decision that determined our salvation. The older we become in the Lord, the more we know it was His choice of us even before the world began. Paul said, in the passage quoted previously, that "He foreknew." Jesus says, "You have not chosen me, I have chosen you" (John 15:16).

Our analogy of a marriage that is true and Christian still holds up. There is a commitment; there is a choice; and there is a promise. Love makes a commitment; love makes a choice; love makes a promise. "For I am very certain that God who began a good work in you will bring it to completion in the Day of Jesus Christ" (Philippians 1:6). God has promised that the beginning He makes in us in a new birth will be brought to fulfillment at the coming of Jesus Christ. The writer of Hebrews reminds his readers that God made a promise to Abraham and God kept that promise by blessing Abraham and multiplying his seed until they were as numberless as the grains of sand at the seashore. He follows this by saying, "In the same way God, desiring even more to show to the heirs of the promise the unchangeableness of His purpose, interposed with an oath, in order that by two unchangeable things, in which it is impossible for God to lie, we may have strong encouragement, we who have fled for refuge in laying hold of the hope set before us. This hope we have as an anchor of the soul, a hope both sure and steadfast." (Hebrews 6:17-19 NASB).

That "we may have strong encouragement . . . God . . interposed by an oath . . . this hope we have as an anchor for the soul." These are all great reassuring statements concerning His promise to us. "For Jesus Christ, the Son of God, who was preached among you by Silas, Timothy and myself, is not the one who is

180

'Yes' and 'No.' On the contrary, He is God's 'Yes'; for it is He who is the 'Yes' to all of God's promises. This is why through Jesus Christ our 'Amen' is said to the glory of God" (II Corinthians 1:19-20 TEV). It is no wonder that we can sing with such confidence, "He has never broken any promise spoken, and He will keep His promise to me." His promise is not easily spoken and quickly forgotten as so many are that are spoken at the marriage altar. He never says, "Well, yes and no." It is always "yes."

A commitment involves action. Love always involves action. Love cannot be passive. "Your eyes have seen all the great acts of the Lord which He did" (Deuteronomy 11:7). "The Lord does righteous acts, and judgments for all who are oppressed. He made known His way to Moses, His acts to the sons of Israel" (Psalms 103:6-7). "Who can speak of the mighty acts of the Lord, or show forth all His praise?" (Psalms 106:2). In a mighty act of deliverance, He redeemed Israel, when they were slaves in Egypt. The Old Testament is indeed a record of the redeeming acts of God in preserving and protecting a people. The climactic act of God in the fulfillment of His eternal purpose was His mighty act in making atonement for man's sin. On that night the world calls Christmas, when the angels sang, *"Gloria in excelsis, gloria,"* Jesus Christ the God-man was born. An old English carol says, "The holly bears a berry as red as any blood, and Mary bore sweet Jesus to do poor sinners good." God's mighty act on behalf of sinning, suffering humanity was the cross. He took sin, suffering and death and nailed them to a cross outside Jerusalem. Yes, God's love acted.

The Word which spoke whole worlds into existence in the beginning was the Word on the cross (John 1:1; I Corinthians 1:18). No wonder the Psalmist said:

The Lord is gracious and merciful;
Slow to anger and great in lovingkindness.

The Lord is good to all,
And His mercies are over all His works,
All Thy works shall give thanks to Thee, O Lord,
And Thy godly ones shall bless Thee.
They shall speak of the glory of Thy kingdom,
And talk of Thy power;
To make known to the sons of men Thy mighty acts,
And the glory of the majesty of Thy kingdom.
Thy kingdom is an everlasting kingdom,
And Thy dominion endures throughout all generations.

(Psalms 145:8-13 NASB)

Love Is Incarnation

We have concluded that, of all of the mighty acts of God in which He committed Himself to us in salvation, the one that literally "blows the mind" is what He did in Jesus Christ.

How can the finite mind grasp the glory of incarnation that "God was in Christ reconciling the world to Himself?" (II Corinthians 5:19). What is the meaning of the baby wrapped in swaddling clothes? What is the meaning of the itinerant preacher-healer who walks dusty road after dusty road preaching, healing and teaching? What is the meaning of the bloody man hanging between heaven and earth? What is the meaning of the empty tomb and the whispered words that passed from mouth to heart and from heart to heart, "He is risen"?

These things mean that God got involved with our world and identified Himself with us in our sin. That God was really here. They mean that God is love. Love gets involved. Love is not ashamed to be identified with its object. "God really cared so much about the world that He gave His only Son" (John 3:16). Either this story is true or we are nothings. We are only some slime that crawled out of some ancient swamp and our only prospect is a nuclear hell that the same slime managed to fashion to destroy itself. If this love story about God is not true, then there is no salvation. And what Stephen Vincent Benét said in his *Burning City* in 1937 is true:

> *You will not be saved by General Motors or*
> *the prefabricated house;*
> *You will not be saved by dialectical materialism,*
> *or the Lambeth conference;*
> *You will not be saved by Vitamin D or*
> *the expanding universe;*
> *In fact you will not be saved.*

Has love cutting into love from above made any difference in our world? When Jonathan Edwards preached his great sermon on "Sinners in the Hands of an Angry God," it is said that men and women came to him while he was still preaching, crying out, "Mr. Edwards, is there any mercy with God?"

If the "rumor of angels," the song they sang over the field of the shepherds, "There is born for you this day in the city of David a Savior which is Christ the Lord," is not true, then there is no hope and we are at the mercy of ourselves. But what our eyes have seen and our hearts have felt and our hands have touched, the very word of life Himself says that it is true. God was in Christ; He lived; He died; He was raised from the dead; He lives at the right hand of God making intercession for us.

The Germans have a word for it, the one mighty act of God, from birth to risen glory, as if taking place in one split second, a second that intersected time—reason cutting into reason, revelation cutting into revelation, love cutting into love, in one mighty act. They call it *Heilsgeschichte,* the "Holy Story."

183

What does that timelessness cutting into time, and eternity invading space and time mean? It means that infinite love, which makes our new birth of love possible, came into a world that had forgotten how to love. God has become involved with us and identified with our hurt, brokenness and sinfulness.

The incarnation and resurrection of Jesus Christ mean that good has triumphed over evil. It is not something that will happen someday; it has already happened. Death, hell and the grave are defeated enemies. Violence may stalk our streets, turning them into jungles of cruelty and inhumanity. Rape may be an ugly word that is featured in everyday's newspaper. Battered children may continue to show up in hospital emergency rooms. Pornographers may continue to sell their poison. The Cosa Nostra may still stick its bloody fingers into every city hall and county courthouse. "The light has shined in the darkness and the darkness cannot put it out." The struggle between light and darkness is not in doubt. That battle was fought and won outside Jerusalem on a bloody cross. God has proclaimed the victim the victor and raised Him from the dead. God's answer to social evil is the church-body. God's answer to cosmic evil is the Christ. The world, the flesh and the Devil are defeated enemies. In Him, we need fear them no longer.

The incarnation and resurrection of Jesus Christ mean that love has triumphed over hate. There are people who, through a new birth, have experienced love cutting into love from above. There are people in Northern Ireland, helpless though they may seem to be in the midst of the horror, whose whole being recoils at what man is doing to man. The same is true in the Middle East. There are people all over this world whose capacity to love has been transformed by the redeeming love of God.

There is real love in human hearts—love that is the deposit of the Spirit. The war between hate and love is not being waged on the battlefields, with guns and bombs. It is being waged in the marketplace, where people with loving hearts made alive in God—in imitation of Jesus Christ—put love into action to touch with sympathy and understanding the ulcerated sores of humanity. Millions live unloved and unloving waiting for that touch of the Spirit.

The battle has already been won. It was won on the cross when He said to those whose spears laid open the heart that loved forever those who hated Him, "Father, forgive them, they do not know what they are doing." Those who have followed Him have found that love is a reality. The lover is a winner! "Love is eternal. Inspired speech is only temporary. Gifts of knowledge and speaking in other languages are only partial gifts and they will pass away. . . . In the meantime three of these will always remain: faith, hope and love. The greatest of these is love" (I Corinthians 13:8-9,13).

The incarnation and resurrection mean that life has triumphed over death. "When . . . this mortal will have put on immortality, then the saying that is true will be fulfilled, 'O death, where is your victory? O death, where is your sting?' The sting of death is sin, and the power of sin is the law; but thanks be to God who gives us the victory in our Lord Jesus Christ" (I Corinthians 15:54-57). Are you afraid of death? Death is a defeated enemy. Paul looked upon death as "being with Christ, which is far better" (Philippians 1:23).

Jesus Christ came into a world that was dead. Man is dead in trespasses and sin. There is no life. The evil is beyond redemption. The indifference to love and God are too deeply embedded in man's nature ever to be eradicated. The greed is too tyrannical and too deeply rooted ever to be destroyed. There is no hope. Then, the first rosy flush of dawn strikes the great stone rolled against the door of the tomb. The dawn

185

comes. The stone is rolled away. Christ is risen! Death is conquered. "Because He lives, we shall live also."

One more chapter remains to be written in that *Heilsgeschichte*. He will return. The great event of the future is the Second Coming of Jesus Christ. It will again be an invasion of time by eternity. The goal of all human history will be attained. The focus of all prophecy will come to bear upon planet earth and its inhabitants. All things will be summed up, completed, brought to fulfillment in Jesus Christ (Ephesians 1:10). This is the event that none of the world's great leaders have even considered in all their deliberations. But the history of man has meaning only in this eternal purpose of God. "And I saw a new heaven and a new earth; for the first heaven and the first earth passed away, and there is no longer any sea. And I saw the holy city, new Jerusalem, coming down out of heaven from God, made ready as a bride adorned for her husband. And I heard a loud voice from the throne, saying, 'Behold the tabernacle of God is among men, and He shall dwell among them, and they shall be His people, and God Himself shall be among them'" (Revelation 21:1-3 NASB).

Those who are His by a new birth will see Him and rejoice. Those who continued to crucify Him with their lovelessness, inhumanity, war, murder, rape, lies and godlessness will "hide from the face of Him that sits upon the throne." There will be no place to hide, for they ignored and rejected the hiding place in the riven side.

Faith, Hope and Love

This section could have been called "Response and Responsibility." How do we make a response to God's love, which is evidenced to us as concern, commitment and incarnation?

God has given us the capacity to receive the love that cuts into all love. God can become our ultimate concern. We can make a commitment to God. Through the mystery of the new birth, Christ can be incarnate in us. The love of God pursues us, but He never forces us to let love in. The giving back of love to love must be a free gift.

We may be afraid of what His love will do to us. Our fear of what lovelessness will do to us should be much greater, for God is love, and lovelessness is hell. What kind of response does His love demand? How do we enter the Kingdom of Love? We respond to concern with concern, to commitment with commitment, to incarnation with incarnation.

"There remain these three: faith, hope and love. The greatest of these is love" (I Corinthians 13:13). These three are clues to how we enter that kingdom. Another clue to response and responsibility is found in the great commandment, "You shall love the Lord your God with all your heart, and with all your soul, and with all your strength, and with all your mind, and your neighbor as yourself" (Luke 10:27; Deuteronomy 6:5; Leviticus 19:18). That is response, to love God—and responsibility, to love man. He asks of us a total commitment of love, involving the whole man, the heart, the mind, the personality, even our physical strength.

We respond to the Father-concern with faith. Believing that God cares about us and loves us is the first step into the love that cuts into love from above. "And without faith it is impossible to please Him, for he who comes to God must believe that He is, and that He is a rewarder of those who seek Him" (Hebrews 11:6 NASB). You can believe. God has given you the capacity for faith. Faith is rejecting our false independence that is slavery. Faith is dethroning self at the center of our being. Faith puts God, His will, His love and His wisdom back in the center of our lives. Faith is rejecting the lie of hell that we are nothing, and accepting God's concern as evidence that we are of infinite worth to God. Faith denies that we are an accident of evolution and affirms that we are the creation of God and made to fellowship with Him. Faith is rejection of the plastic gods that are not gods and acceptance of the Father God who loves and cares. Faith is leaving our doubts and believing the promises of God. Faith is both an affirmation and an act. Faith affirms God as concern. Faith acts by submitting the will to God. It is the will to believe that saves. Faith is the only door into the new birth experience with God. "For by grace you have been saved through faith; and that not of yourselves, it is the gift of God" (Ephesians 2:8 NASB).

We respond to the Father's commitment to us with hope. His commitment to us was pledged in Jesus Christ. Before the new birth we were "without God and without hope in the world" (Ephesians 2:12). Paul gives his benediction to the Christians in Thessalonica, "Now may our Lord Jesus Christ Himself and God our Father, who has loved us and given us eternal comfort and good hope by grace, comfort and strengthen your hearts in every good work and word" (II Thessalonians 2:16,17 NASB). The word "hope" in the New Testament occurs most often in connection with the resurrection of the people of God, the redemption of the body and the return of Jesus Christ. If we have been born again, we are not constantly wringing our hands about world conditions. We know that the hope of the believer and the world is in Jesus Christ. We know He has "the whole world in His hands." When hope is a reality in our lives, there will be joy. "We rejoice in the hope of the glory of God" (Romans 5:2); "Now may the God of hope fill you with all joy" (Romans 15:13); "Rejoicing in hope" (Romans 12:12). This is the reason early Christians could face wild cattle and lions in the Roman arenas with singing and praise. They had hope and hope gave joy. In our own time, the revival in the early 1970s that we call "the Jesus Revolution" came out of a response to hope in Jesus Christ. Youth had tried everything and found it hopeless; they found joy in their hope in Jesus Christ. They, too, called it a new birth.

Love is the response to His love cutting into our loves. Love is related to the incarnation because love is incarnational. It was love that made the Word flesh. Our response to Him is incarnational love. His love is returned to Him. God, who is love, is loved by us. We love Him with the love that came from Him to us. He came into our world. He has come into our innermost being. The whole man responds to His love by loving. We love Him with our minds, our bodies and our will. The lesson of Calvary is clear—sin can hurt God. It is the nature of love to protect its beloved. Because sin hurts God, love casts out sin. "Love casts out fear," and fear is sin. The deepest expression of this response of love to God is that we no longer want to hurt Him with our sins.

I repeat the example of the father I assisted in getting his son out of a jam with the police. We waited in a room for the boy to be brought to us. While we were waiting, the father broke down and began sobbing and weeping. An officer brought the boy in. He stood there looking at his father and hearing him weep. The father was so broken up that he did not know the boy was in the room. The boy ran to his father and began crying and, at the same time, saying, "Oh Daddy, forgive me. I didn't know you cared so much." The Father cares that much. "We love Him because He first loved us." The new birth is the beginning of the life of faith, hope and love.

Our responsibility begins when new life begins. "Love your neighbor as yourself." The parable of the good Samaritan establishes that our neighbor is anyone who has a need (Luke 10:25-37). Attitudes are basic in our relationship to God, but actions are basic in our relationships to man. I can love God. I can worship God. I can adore and praise God. I cannot give God a cup of cold water. I cannot put God up for the night. I cannot be a big brother or big sister to God. I cannot speak kindly to God. All of these actions must be done on behalf of God to others.

All around us are people who suffer from alienation, brokenness, vicious habits and oppressive injustices. They hurt. I must be the love of God incarnate to them. Born again believers today, in many churches, are discovering their grace-gifts and are using them in ministry to people within and without the church. They are incarnating love to people in hospitals, nursing homes, homes for the elderly, jails, prisons and mental institutions. God does not need any more armchair social reformers who write great books and make great speeches on how much society needs to be reformed but never get involved personally. God got involved in our world. Knowing and loving God is getting involved in sharing in the brokenness of our world. It is concern for the world. It is commitment to a healing, reconciling ministry. It is incarnating His love. If we are born of God, we are made in His likeness. That's what it's all about— Christlikeness. May He be born in you, the hope of glory. May He live in you, the hope of humanity.

What has happened to me? Just a week ago Bill and I prayed together. I received Jesus Christ as Lord and Savior. I am different and I am not different. The things that I did before, I don't enjoy when I do them now. Things that I never used to enjoy I look forward to, like that prayer meeting tonight in the dormitory. Who would ever have thought I would look forward to a prayer meeting? Tomorrow I am going to church with the people from the meeting.

I never could understand the Bible before, but I really got a lot out of the Bible study group last night in Joe's room. I wonder if it will last? I can't wait to tell Mom and Dad what happened to me. They are not Christians. I never was concerned about them before. I think I will write them a letter and sort of prepare the way for when I come home. Maybe I can influence them. Bill said I could pray for them.

Bill called it "born again." I sure have done some new things, for me—praying and all that. It is really good, though. It does seem to be a different world—better, nicer, cleaner. "Clean" is the word. I felt so clean when Bill and I finished praying. Lord, I do thank you for changing my life and for helping me get it all together. It's good to be born again. It's like a brand new world. It's better than smoking pot—no more of that stuff for me. I'm a new me, and it is good.

8.

NOW THAT YOU'VE BEEN BORN AGAIN

"And they sailed to the country of the Gerasenes, which is opposite Galilee. And when He had come out onto the land, a certain man from the city met Him who was possessed with demons; and who had not put on any clothing for a long time, and was not living in a house, but in the tombs. And seeing Jesus, he cried out and fell before Him, and said in a loud voice, 'What do I have to do with You, Jesus, Son of the Most High God? I beg You, do not torment me.' . . .

"And Jesus asked him, 'What is your name?' And he said, 'Legion'; for many demons had entered him. . . . Now there was a herd of many swine feeding there on the mountain. . . . And the demons came out from the man and entered the swine; and the herd rushed down the steep bank into the lake, and were drowned.

"And when those who tended them saw what had happened, they ran away and reported it in the city and out in the country. And the people went out to see what had happened; and they came to Jesus, and found the man from whom the demons had gone out, sitting down at the feet of Jesus, clothed and in his right mind; and they became frightened. . . .

"And all the people of the country of Gerasenes and the surrounding district asked Him to depart from them; for they were gripped with great fear; and He got into a boat, and returned. But the man from whom the demons had gone out was begging Him that he might accompany Him; but He sent him away saying, 'Return to your house and describe what great things God has done for you.' And he departed, proclaiming throughout the whole city what great things Jesus had done for him" (Luke 8:26-39 NASB).

I like very much the TV commercial in which small children are interviewed and asked, "What do you want to do when you grow up?" One boy, about five or six years old, says he is going to buy a boat and a train and an airplane and then he is going to see the whole world, "as soon as my mother lets me cross the street." You do have to learn to cross the street before you can see the world. It is all a matter of growing up.

Growing up is as much a part of the spiritual life as of our natural lives. It was true of Jesus. "And Jesus kept increasing in wisdom and stature, and in favor with God and men." Jesus grew physically, mentally, socially and spiritually. You may have been born again at twenty or thirty or forty years of age and, from the time of your spiritual birth, you began your spiritual growth. The author of the epistle to the Hebrews urged new Christians to get off baby food and onto the solid food of the word of righteousness so that they would become mature Christians. "For every one who partakes only of milk is not accustomed to the word of righteousness, for he is a babe. But solid food is for the mature, who because of practice have their senses trained to discern good and evil. Therefore leaving the

193

elementary teaching about the Christ, let us press on to maturity" (Hebrews 5:13-6:1 NASB). As a babe in Christ, you know Him as Lord and Savior. Now that you know Him, there is the whole world of spiritual reality to know and understand. Let's get on with it.

Is the thrill of the once-for-all experience of being born again all there is? Is the new birth a spiritual jag that solves no problems, answers no questions and brings no continuing experiences? Living is more than being born. All you have done in the new birth is cross the street. Before you lie the joy and pain of growing up, of enjoying and exploring God's great world of spiritual reality and truth. A whole spiritual lifetime of growing up in Jesus Christ lies ahead.

It is wonderful to be a child. My seven-year-old grandson called me long distance to tell me about his being in a demonstration of tumbling that his school gave for the parents. He said excitedly, "Grandad, I couldn't believe I was so good." There was no ego in it, only the pure joy of living. It is as great a tragedy to remain a child as it is wonderful to be a child. How many of the thirty-four per cent of the American adult public who claim to have experienced a new birth are still babies in Christ? How many are still on milk when they should have been bottle broken long ago. Only eighteen per cent of the adult American public say they witness regularly to their faith and try to bring others to that faith. A large number who claim the new birth have not yet found it comfortable to share their faith in Jesus Christ. They have not grown up. "You therefore, beloved, knowing this beforehand, be on your guard lest, being carried away by the error of unprincipled men, you fall from your own steadfastness, but grow in the grace and knowledge of our Lord and Saviour Jesus Christ. To Him be the glory, both now and to the day of eternity. Amen" (II Peter 3:17,18 NASB).

In the King James version of the Scriptures, Luke

says that Jesus told the demoniac of Gadara to go home and "show" what great things the Lord had done for him. The same version says that Mark says Jesus told him to go home and "tell" the great things the Lord had done for him. This is exactly what growing up in Christ is all about. It is demonstrating Christ-likeness in your life and sharing verbally what He has done for you.

The name of the game is "Show and Tell." It is a game most of us have heard about. Children play the game at school. On an announced day, all the children bring something to school and, when they are called upon, they show the class what they have brought and tell the class about it. They may bring a stamp collection, a pet lizard, or some other treasured possession. The demoniac, now healed and in his right mind, wants to go and travel with Jesus so he can tell the great crowds following the Savior what has happened to him. Jesus tells him he cannot go with Him, that he must go home where people know him, and show and tell them the good news. He must be the good news and verbalize the good news. It is "Show and Tell" day for this man made new in Jesus Christ. It is "Show and Tell" day for you.

The new birth is not referred to in the account of the transformation of the demoniac, yet, if ever a man was reborn, it is this man. Are demons a reality in our world today? The demons of alcoholism, drug addiction, pride, greed, criticism, gossip and lying are very real today. None of these demons enter our lives without our permission. This man has to say, "Am I possessed with demons? You name the demon and I've got it." When he is reborn, he is "sitting there, clothed, and in his right mind." He is now calm; he is decent; and he is at peace with himself because he is at peace with God. His mind is no longer tormented. He's got it all together. Now that he is a new man, what is he to do?

Jesus tells him to go home and show in all the relationships of life that he is a new man. He will be a new husband for his wife. He will be a new father for his children. He will be a new citizen for his community. He is to tell what has happened to him and all about the Person who changed his life. When they ask, "Sam, what on earth has happened to you?" He will be ready to tell. "But sanctify Christ as Lord in your hearts, always being ready to make a defense to every one who asks you to give an account for the hope that is in you, yet with gentleness and reverence" (I Peter 3:15 NASB).

There is really no way that you can tell without showing. The Word must become flesh. What Christ said and did while He was here must become flesh and blood in your life. No one (not even God) expects you to be perfect, but everyone (including God) expects you to be different. If Christ has made no difference in your life, there is every reason to believe that you have never been born again. Why ask people to believe if our belief makes no difference in our lives? Most people agree that they would rather see a sermon than hear one. Jesus said, "I am saying to you that if your righteousness is not any better than that of the Scribes and Pharisees, you will never enter the kingdom of heaven" (Matthew 5:20). The Scribes and Pharisees were very religious, but Jesus said they neglected love, justice and faithfulness (Matthew 23:23). They had a list of things that you could do and things you couldn't do. It was their own list and they became the judges of everyone who did not do exactly as they did.

If you do not practice what you preach, you will hear the world saying, "Physician, heal thyself." The gospel must show in your life. Believers must *be* the gospel as well as preach the gospel. Shouting out the gospel a little louder will not substitute for right living and loving concern for others. Holy living is always impressive and contagious. If you do not live the good news, you will be like the pastor Shakespeare wrote about in Hamlet:

> Do not as some ungracious pastors do,
> Show me the steep and thorny way to heaven,
> Whiles like a puff'd and reckless libertine,
> Himself the primrose path of dalliance treads,
> And recks not his own rede.

Many people are not able to share their faith verbally because they know that their lives are not in line with what they believe. A pastor asked me to meet with the deacons of his church before a series of special meetings we were going to conduct there. He asked me to prepare the deacons for evangelistic visitation in which they would share their faith with persons who were not Christians. I had hardly begun my presentation when a young deacon interrupted me and said, "I am not going to do this. This is not my work. I think this is something that you and the pastor should do and not me. I refuse to do it."

The pastor answered, "Terry, let's let Brother John finish his presentation and then tomorrow morning you and I can talk about this. I think we can reach an understanding."

The pastor shared with me the next day his conversation with Terry earlier that morning. The pastor said, "Terry, I think there is something bothering you. I really don't believe that you mean what you said. There is something else wrong. Do you want to share it with me? I will understand whatever it is." Terry began crying. When he had control of himself, he said, "Pastor, you know I coach football at the high school. Everyone knows me. The boys all know that my language hasn't been right. I have been cursing before the boys. I have done some other things that are not right when we have been on trips with the teams. I can't go out and share my faith with others. There are too many people who know me. My life just doesn't measure up." Unfortunately, not everyone who is a church member realizes as clearly as Terry the stumbling block they become when their lives are not what they should be.

I met a railroad worker in a small hotel and, after we had become friends, talked to him about becoming a Christian. He said, "Now don't talk to me about being a Christian. The last time I took a trip, one member of the crew entertained us on the whole trip with dirty stories. He cursed worse than I do. When I got back to town, I decided I would go to church. That morning they had communion and guess who served the bread and wine? That same guy! No, don't talk to me about church. I am never going back again."

A church member who may never have experienced the new birth was a stumbling block because his life in the world did not measure up to his service in the church. It takes real discipline to live the life worth sharing. It is not easy to be a demonstration of what Christ can do for a person. "Therefore be imitators of God, as beloved children; and walk in love, just as Christ also loved you, and gave Himself up for us, an offering and a sacrifice to God as a fragrant aroma. But do not let immorality or any impurity or greed even be named among you, as is proper among saints; and there must be no filthiness and silly talk, or coarse jesting, which are not fitting, but rather giving of thanks" (Ephesians 5:1-4 NASB).

It is just as true that you cannot show without telling. It is difficult to "go home and tell what great things the Lord has done for you." "But Peter and John answered and said to them, 'Whether it is right in the sight of God to give heed to you rather than to God, you be the judge; for we cannot stop speaking what we have seen and heard'" (Acts 4:19,20

NASB). The man who is without Christ and is honest about himself admits that he is not as good as some. He says, "I am just weak. I wish that I were as good as James, who says he has been born again. He is strong and lives a good life. But I'm just not like that."

He will go on believing that the difference between himself and James is goodness. Not until James, who is born again, goes to him and says, "Fred, I am just like you are. I am a sinner, too. The difference is that Jesus Christ helps me to be what I need to be. If you let Him in your life, He can help you, too." It is wrong for us to think that, just by living a good life, we are doing all that the Lord expects of us. He expects us to play the game, to show and tell. "But having the same spirit of faith, according to what is written, 'I believed, therefore I spoke,' we also believe, therefore also we speak; . . . For all things are for your sakes, that the grace which is spreading to more and more people may cause the giving of thanks to abound to the glory of God" (II Corinthians 4:13-15 NASB).

Nothing can explain the sweeping evangelism of the early Christians except the power of the Holy Spirit and the power of personal testimony. People experienced new life in Christ and shared what that experience meant in their lives. By the end of the first century, the faith had spread into the whole world. By the end of the third century, whole empires were laid at the feet of the crucified Nazarene and a dying Roman emperor was to say with his last breath, "Galilean, thou hast conquered."

Now that you've been born again, you are enrolled in the school of Christ and there are just two subjects, showing and telling. Because you are something, you have something to say. Theology, denominations, church buildings, rituals, ceremonies, priests, parsons and ecclesiastical officials mean nothing unless there are lives that have been skillfully delivered from the kingdom of sin and graciously remade into fit subjects for the Kingdom of God. The demoniac of Gadara was dramatically and thrillingly changed by Jesus Christ and charged to show and tell—to his relatives, to his community—what Jesus Christ had done in his life. You have the same responsibility.

Am I Really a New Person?

You are a miracle. The greatest miracle of the twentieth or any other century. You are a miracle of the new birth. Every child born naturally of its parents is a miracle, a miracle of life. You are born of God and you are a miracle, a miracle of birth from above. "That which is born of the flesh is flesh, and that which is born of the Spirit is spirit" (John 3:6). What has happened in your life defies any physical or psychological explanation. You now possess a life so new, so revolutionary and so different that it is like being born all over again.

Now you have the right to be called a son of God. "Every one who has received Him, the ones believing on His name, He gave the right to be children of God—children who were born not of natural birth or human decision—but of God" (John 1:12,13).

The spiritual birth has given you spiritual life. As in all life, it will require nourishment, exercise and tender loving care. This does not mean that all your problems are solved. For many people, being born again brings many new problems. There will now be a struggle within you between self and the new spiritual nature. As the spiritual life is nourished and grows, it will be easier for you to live in the spirit and deny the things that self wants. "He condemned sin in the flesh, in order that the requirements of the Law might be

200

fulfilled in us who do not walk according to the flesh, but according to the Spirit. For those who are according to the flesh set their minds on the things of the flesh, but those who are according to the Spirit, the things of the Spirit" (Romans 8:3-5 NASB).

You are a new person. You are a new person because Christ has come to live in your heart by faith. "That He would grant you, according to the riches of His glory, to be strengthened with power through His spirit in the inner man; so that Christ may dwell in your hearts by faith; and that you, being rooted and grounded in love, may know with all the people of God . . . the love of Christ which surpasses knowledge" (Ephesians 3:16-19). Jesus promised, in the upper room before He went away to be with the Father, that the Helper, the Holy Spirit, would come and cause the reality of Christ's living in your life to become a present accepted reality. "After a little while the world shall see Me no more; but you will see Me; because I live you will also live. When that day comes you will know that I am in the Father, and you in Me, and I in you" (John 14:19,20). In His death and resurrection, He changed His body from that body given to Him by the Holy Spirit in the womb of the Virgin for a new body, the church. He lives in every born again believer. You accept this by faith. Because He lives in us, our lives are no longer our own to live in self-will. You have become His. You belong to Him (I Corinthians 6:20).

Your eyes are new so that you see His world through His eyes. Your lips are new to take His name with purpose and power. Your hands are new to do His work of love and compassion. Your mind is new to think as He thinks.

Do you remember Nancy Howell in the first chapter of this book? She said, in describing the new birth, that "life is more joyous, the sky bluer, the grass

201

greener, people lovelier." You begin to see the world from His eyes.

> *Heaven above is softer blue,*
> *Earth around is sweeter green,*
> *Something lives in every hue,*
> *Christless eyes have never seen.*
> *Birds with gladder songs o'erflow,*
> *Flowers with deeper beauty shine,*
> *Since I know—as now I know—*
> *That I am His and He is mine.*

You are a new person because He is now in control. Henry Drummond, the great preacher, was a very sensitive seeker of people who were not Christians. One day he took a public horse-drawn coach and, rather than sitting in the coach, he asked the driver if he could sit on the seat above the coach with him. The driver gave him permission and soon Drummond was pressing the claims of Christ on the coachman. The man was reluctant to surrender to Christ because of a habit by which he was bound and didn't feel capable of giving up even though he knew it was wrong. Drummond asked him, "Suppose your horses ran away and you lost control of them and they were racing wild down a steep hill. What could you do?"

The man said, "If I lost control of them, I guess I would be helpless."

"Just suppose," said Drummond, "that beside you was sitting the greatest driver of horses in the world, who was much stronger and more capable than you. What would you do then?"

The man said, "I would give the reins to him."

"Of course," replied Drummond, "you would give him the reins. Your life is out of control. This vicious habit that is ruining your life always controls you. Here beside you is the Lord Jesus Christ. He is

202

stronger than you. He conquered temptation. Will you give the reins of your life to Him?"

The man did give his life to Jesus Christ and found victory in Christ. That is exactly what has happened to you. You have given Jesus Christ the controls in your life. You have given Him control of your life, now trust Him to direct your life daily. Once you were controlled by money or sex or pride or self. Now He is in control.

The God who lives in you has chosen to reveal Himself as Father, Son and Holy Spirit. Philip, one of the disciples, asked Jesus to show him the Father. Jesus answered, "Do you not believe that I am in the Father and the Father is in Me? The words that I am saying to you now I am not speaking on my own initiative. . . . Believe Me that I am in the Father, and the Father in Me. . . . And I will ask the Father, and He will give another Helper, that He may be with you always. . . . He is the Helper, the Holy Spirit whom the Father will send in my name. He will teach you all things, and bring to your remembrance all the things I said to you" (John 14:10,11,16,26).

As Father, God nourishes His life in us. He cares for us and we can go to Him for help and hope. As Son, Jesus Christ, God has saved us and given us a flesh and blood revelation of Himself and how we are to live. As Holy Spirit, the Helper, God lives in us and does exactly what His name suggests. He helps. He gives us the guidance we need. He helps us to know what we should ask of the Father in prayer. He strengthens us in our weakness. "In the same way the Holy Spirit also helps us in our weaknesses; for we do not know how to pray, but the Spirit Himself pleads for the saints according to the will of God" (Romans 8:26).

A teacher of the law had asked Jesus which commandment was the most important, and Jesus said, "Listen, Israel, the Lord our God is one Lord. Love the Lord your God with all your heart" (Mark 12:29).

There is only one God who lives in us. God has chosen to reveal Himself to us as Father, Son and Holy Spirit. You are a new person in Him.

How Long Will It Last?

You have eternal life. The word "eternal" means the kind of life you have and its duration. You have been born again and you are His child forever. It is interesting that the New Testament uses both "birth" and "adoption" to refer to our being the children of God. The word "birth" relates to our having the characteristics of God. We are like our parents because we have the genes of our parents. The word "adoption" is used to relate to our being God's children because, under law, in the Greco-Roman world, an adopted child could not be disinherited. This is also true of the law in many of the states in the United States. Our only daughter is adopted and I took an oath never to disinherit her.

"No one who is born of God keeps on practicing sin, because His seed is in him." As born again children of God, the seed of God (characteristics passed on to us) remains in us. "God sent His Son to free us from the law, that we might be adopted as sons. . . . Because of that you are no longer a slave but a son, and if you are a son, you are an heir through God" (Galatians 4:4,5,7). We are qualified to share in the inheritance of the saints (Colossians 1:12). You are a born again and adopted child of God.

There are people who live in the fear that, once having been saved, they can again be lost. They live in constant torment in which they really never know their real standing before God. Can you imagine a good parent saying to a five-year-old child, who has just told his first lie, "You are no longer my child. You have lied.

I will no longer support you. It is cold and raining outside, but you must leave the house and never come back." Not only would this be a poor parent, but he or she could be prosecuted for child abuse. If God were like that, He would not even be as good and loving as a human parent must be, according to the demands of our society. Can someone be "unborn" once he is born? Can a child be disinherited when that child has received "the adoption of children"? Everything that Jesus taught us about God cries out against that view of God. How can this kind of relationship with a child be squared with the waiting Father in Luke 15? The life of God that is in you is eternal life. Does God play tricks on us in saying, "I give you eternal life and you shall never perish," only to take it back when we stray?

It is this very kind of life and love that keeps us from straying and keeps us in the Father's love. Indeed, for you to believe that you can be lost after you are found would be an encouragement for you to sin and then say, "Well, I can always be saved again." You cannot play with the grace of God like that. Paul says, "I am convinced that neither death, nor life, nor angels, nor principalities, nor things present, nor things to come, nor powers, nor height, nor depth, nor any other created thing, shall be able to separate us from the love of God, which is in Christ Jesus our Lord" (Romans 8:38,39 NASB).

Our eternal life is based on the promise of God. He will never play games with you. "In hope of eternal life which God, who cannot lie, promised ages ago" (Titus 1:2). God cannot lie. God has promised you eternal life and, if it is anything less than eternal, God has broken His promise to you. But He will not break His word. Israel had sinned against God and He could have destroyed them. There is a verse given to us by the prophet Malachi which is very revealing: "I am the Lord, I do not change. Therefore you sons of Jacob are not destroyed" (Malachi 3:6). God said, "I made a promise to Abraham and I will keep my promise." The promise of God to give you eternal life is based on His character.

We sing, "How firm a foundation ye saints of the Lord, was laid by your faith in His excellent Word." The foundation of our hope is the character of God who does not lie. Our present faith in His promise to give us eternal life is in the promises of God in the Bible. "God loved the world so much that He gave His only begotten Son so that whoever believes in Him shall not perish but have eternal life" (John 3:16). You either believe or you do not believe it. God either lies or tells the truth. "For you have died and your life is hidden with Christ in God. When Christ, who is our life, shall appear, then you also will appear with Him in glory" (Colossians 3:3,4). Your eternal life is in Christ and in God and is safe until He comes and all His own appear with Him in glory. That is God's promise to you.

If you have only human life, then it can be taken by yourself or by disease or by someone else. If you have God's life in you, it is safe in Him. "Now to Him who is able to keep you from stumbling, and to make you stand in the presence of His glory blameless with great joy, to the only God our Savior, through Jesus Christ our Lord, be glory, dominion and authority, before all time and now and forever" (Jude 24-25). It is His ability and not yours that you must count on. The life that you have will last forever. It could not be clearer than "before all time, and now, and forever."

Will you ever doubt that you have eternal life? Yes, you will doubt it. One of the ways the Tempter has of getting into our lives is to raise doubts about the goodness of God and our relationship to Him. This is what the Satan did with Even in the garden. "Has God really said that? Now, can you imagine God saying that? Is He really good? He surely didn't mean that." The Satan raises questions in our minds about God. Children who think they are treated unfairly by their parents often have fantasies about not really belonging to their parents: "The way they are treating me, I must not really belong to them." When doubts are in our minds, we must go back to the promises. Faith is never stronger than when it is forged in the depths of doubt. In Dwight Moody's Bible, there appeared the following words: "God said it, I believe it, that settles it."

Will I Still Have Temptations?

Yes, you will still have temptations. God has promised His strength and grace to resist temptation if you will claim it by faith. Paul is writing to Christians and he says, "No temptation has overtaken you but such as is common to man; and God is faithful, who will not allow you to be tempted beyond what you are able, but with the temptation will provide the way of escape also, that you may be able to endure it" (I Corinthians 10:13 NASB). First, it is helpful for you to remember that the temptations you experience are temptations that others are facing. Your victory over temptation will help others to overcome their temptation. Second, God will not allow you to be tempted beyond your ability. You can always say to yourself, "Now, this is a temptation. But God knows I have the ability to resist the temptation. I thank Him because He has confidence in me, in allowing me to be in this position." Third, God always makes a way of escape. You can say, "Now, Lord, I know that there is a way for me to get out of this situation. Help me to know and recognize it and use it to your glory."

Remember that He was tempted in every way that we are tempted, and yet He never sinned. The writer

207

of Hebrews says that we have a "merciful and faithful high priest" (one who intercedes for us) in Jesus Christ, "For since He Himself was tempted in that which He has suffered, He is able to come to the aid of those who are tempted" (Hebrews 2:18 NASB). If you had to go to someone for help when you were tempted, would you rather go to someone who had faced the same temptation and had a victory over it or someone who had never been tempted in the same way as you? I think we would all like to go to someone who knows what it means to wear our shoes. He is never shocked by how bad we are and he is never surprised by how good we are. All he expects of us is honesty about ourselves. "For we do not have a high priest who cannot sympathize with our weaknesses, but one who has been tempted in all things as we are, yet without sin" (Hebrews 4:15 NASB).

When you are tempted, pray. Right there, wherever you are, you can say to God, "Father, I am being tempted. I know others have been tempted just as I am. I know some of them had the victory. I know that you are now allowing me to be tempted beyond my ability to resist. Help me to see the way of escape you have provided for me. Father, I know our Savior was tempted and I know He never sinned. Now help me to be like Him. Give me His strength." Because we have that high priest who knows how to sympathize and who has been tempted as we are, "Let us draw near with confidence to the throne of grace, that we may receive mercy and may find grace to help in the time of need" (Hebrews 4:16 NASB).

The difference between someone who has been born again and someone who has not is not that one never sins and the other one does. The difference is in the attitude that we have toward our sins. A man was cursing and swearing, one obscenity after the other coming from his mouth. A new Christian, who had just recently been born again, said to him, "I used to curse and swear like that. It really hurts me now to hear you use God's name like that. I wish you wouldn't do it."

The man cursed again and said, "I'll have you know that I am a deacon in the church and I believe 'once saved, always saved.' If I want to curse, I'll do it." He had never been born again. If a person has been born again, he cannot have that kind of attitude about his sins. Now that you are God's child, you will have guilt for your sins and the Lord will chasten you for your sins. "For those whom the Lord loves He disciplines, and He punishes every son whom He receives" (Hebrews 12:6). We can rejoice in God's discipline because it is an indication that we are His children.

You can nip sin in the bud by resisting temptation. Evil desire leads to lust and lust leads to sin. Someone has said, "You cannot keep the birds from flying over your head, but you can keep them from building nests in your hair." You may be asking, "Why does God allow me to be tempted at all?" God wants men and women and youths, who are morally strong, not puppets forced to do His will. "It is for discipline that you endure [temptation and God's chastening if you sin]; God deals with you as sons; for what son is there who is not disciplined by his father? For if you are not disciplined in this way, you are not children at all" (Hebrews 12:7,8). Part of the discipline that the Father expects us to endure is to face temptation and overcome it. Every time we successfully resist temptation, we become morally stronger. Every time we succumb to temptation, we become morally weaker. That law is as inexorable and unchanging as the tides and the sunrise. God does not want to lead into that fuller and larger life of glory a host of moral cripples. It is for this reason that the Scriptures say, "Be strong in the Lord in the strength of His power. Put on all the armor of God that you may be able to resist evil, that you may be able to stand against all the tricks of the Devil" (Ephesians 6:10,11).

209

How Can I Understand the Bible?

There are many things in the Bible that I do not understand after studying it more than thirty years. Sometimes, God, through His Holy Spirit, gives me some light on Bible passages that have been a mystery to me for many years. There are some things that can help you in your understanding of the Bible.

The first thing is to get a copy of the Bible in modern English or Spanish or whatever language you read best. The *Good News Bible: Today's English Version* is available in either English or Spanish from the American Bible Society. A better translation, but a little more difficult to read, is *The New American Standard Bible*. It is available in most bookstores.

Begin your reading in either Luke's gospel or John's gospel. Do not read the Scriptures for content, read them for action. What the Bible says is not nearly so important as how it applies to your life. Many people have studied the Bible for years, but remember very little because they didn't put it into practice. We may run across a verse that says, "Happy are the pure in heart, for they shall see God." How can I be pure in heart today? If I am pure in heart, in what way will I see God? Then you try it in your experience and see how it works. Live and practice what you do understand and wait for God to give you more light on what you do not understand.

Some of the Bible is difficult to understand because it is written in ideas and thought forms of a culture different from ours. For instance, "Abraham's bosom" is "heaven" to us. A "wineskin" is a "bottle" to us. There are thousands of words that have different meanings today. Fortunately, the modern English versions

210

put most of these words in the vocabulary of today. The Bible also uses some very figurative language because it was the way people expressed themselves in those times. The Bible may speak poetically of the "mountains skipping for joy" or the "moon turning to blood." Some of the natural phenomena were seen as portents of doom and judgment and these kinds of concepts are used to communicate the judgments of God in the Scriptures. Parts of the Bible were written during times of persecution and harassment for Christians and sometimes the real message may have been deliberately concealed so that only Christians could understand the message of the writer.

Take the great simple passages and memorize them. Put them into practice. For a Christian, there is no substitute for the Word of God, read, memorized and lived out. "How can a young man keep his way pure? By keeping it according to Thy Word. With all my heart I have sought Thee; do not let me wander from Thy commandments. Thy Word have I treasured in my heart, that I may not sin against Thee" (Psalms 119: 9-11).

Study the Bible in the company of other people who, like you, are searching for knowledge of the Scriptures. Another person, perhaps the person who was used of God in helping you to experience the new birth, may be able to meet you for an hour or two several times a week for Bible study. When you study the Bible with others, it is more enjoyable and you can help each other as you search for truth in the Word of God. Many high schools and college dormitories have Bible study groups that you can discover by asking around. Often, there are informal Bible study groups of women meeting in apartment complexes and senior citizen developments. Bible classes meet every Sunday in most churches and you can find fellowship with people who love to study the Bible. Christian colleges and seminaries often offer night classes and correspondence courses in the Bible which may be quite helpful.

The most important thing for your Bible study is a regular time to read from the Psalms and the gospels for your own spiritual food. A quiet time alone with God and the Scriptures is an indispensable part of Christian living. This time, with no one else present, will become one of the greatest experiences of your Christian life. Remember that the Holy Spirit, who lives within you, is the best Bible teacher you could possibly find. Remember that Jesus said He would send the Helper to help you remember and understand all that Jesus said and did. That is what the Bible is about. "Now we have received, not the spirit of the world, but the Spirit who is from God, that we might know the things freely given to us by God, which things we also speak, not in words taught by human wisdom, but in those taught by the Spirit, combining spiritual thoughts with spiritual words" (I Corinthians 2:12,13).

How Can I Talk to God?

Prayer is the verb of Christian living. Prayer is action. Prayer is asking and receiving. Jesus says for us to "Ask and you shall receive; seek and you shall find; knock and the door will be opened" (Luke 11:9). It is interesting that the first letter in each of the three phrases spell "ask." As the moon depends on the sun for every bit of its radiance, as the branch depends on the vine for every bit of its life and fruit, as the lamp depends on the power plant for its brightness, we depend on God for everything we are and have. Isn't it reasonable, then, that we talk with Him?

You can talk with God, and the more you talk with Him, the more you become like Him. There is a great deal of our praying that we must do amid all the routine of life. Gerhardt Ter Steegen has expressed this need well:

His priest am I, before Him day and night,
  Within His Holy Place;
And death, and life, and all things dark and bright,
  I spread before His Face.
Rejoicing with His joy, yet ever still,
  For silence is my song;
My work to bend beneath His blessed will.
  And day, and all night long,
For ever holding with Him converse sweet,
Yet speechless, for my gladness is complete.

The Bible includes many prayers that you can use as models for your praying. The prayer of praise and adoration is a time when you are not asking the Father for something, but you are just telling Him how much you love Him and why you adore Him, expressing your praise of Him as your God and Father. One prayer like that is the prayer of David: "I will extol Thee, my God, O King; and I will bless Thy name forever and ever. Every day will I bless Thee, and I will praise Thy name forever and ever. Great is the Lord, and highly to be praised; and His greatness is unsearchable. One generation shall praise Thy works to another, and shall declare Thy mighty acts. On the glorious splendor of Thy majesty, and on Thy wonderful works, I will meditate" (Psalms 145:1-5 NASB).

A prayer of penitence is a prayer for forgiveness for sin. It is an admission of guilt and a request for cleansing and pardon. A good model is the prayer of David: "Be gracious to me, O God, according Thy lovingkindness; according to the greatness of Thy compassion blot out my transgressions. Wash me thoroughly from my iniquity, and cleanse me from my sin. For I know my transgressions, and my sin is ever before me. Against Thee, Thee only, I have sinned, and done what is evil in Thy sight, so that Thou art justified when Thou dost speak, and blameless when Thou dost judge" (Psalms 51:1-4 NASB).

Some of the things you need to pray for every day are indicated in the model prayer that Jesus taught the disciples. You need to pray for food to eat, for forgiveness of your sins and the ability to forgive others. You need to pray daily for deliverance from temptation (Luke 11:1-4). The prayers of Paul in Ephesians, Colossians, and Philippians are great prayers that were prayed for fellow believers. Studying these prayers in the Scriptures will help you to know how to pray.

You may find that a prayer group or a prayer partner can assist you in beginning your prayer life. Some Christians with whom you work might agree with you to be your "prayer partner." You can share some of the things that you agree you want to pray for and at a designated time you can pray together in the same place or simultaneously in different places. Some people have become "telephone prayer partners." In this case, you meet your prayer partner at a given time on the telephone, sharing your prayer requests, then each of you leading in a brief prayer time. There are groups of Christians who meet regularly to pray for specific things, such as a revival in America, the needs of missionaries, or world hunger and world evangelism. People who are shut-in by illness or infirmity are often enlisted by churches as intercessors for specific needs and requests. Many churches have prayer groups that consider prayer their special ministry and have specific times when the group meets to pray for requests that have come from radio and TV listeners and or persons in the church and the community.

Prayer is actually a method in evangelism. One of

the ways that we can really touch the lives of others is through the mystery of prayer. Prayer is the power "that moves the hand that moves the world to bring salvation down." When our friends and relatives will not allow us to talk to them about their need of Christ, we can still pray. One of the greatest revivals I have ever experienced was in a community in Missouri. A man almost eighty years old became a child of God by the new birth. When he came to make his public profession of faith in Christ, his wife gave her testimony and said, "For fifty years I have prayed for my husband. I prayed for him every day. I never quit believing that someday he would become a Christian. Today it has happened, and I praise God." A revival of religion began in that community resulting in the rebirth of hundreds of people. You can keep a prayer list of your relatives and friends who are not Christians and use that prayer list to remind you to pray for them. You can have the joy of crossing them off that list as they are, one by one, born again.

How Can I Be a Witness?

You can be a witness by showing and telling. Every Christian is a witness. Our witness may be good or bad, but it is there. What we do and what we say either witnesses to Christ or it detracts from the power of the Christian witness. "But you shall receive power when the Holy Spirit has come upon you; and you shall be My witnesses both in Jerusalem, and in all Judea and Samaria, and even to the remotest part of the earth" (Acts 1:8 NASB). To witness is to give credible testimony to the transforming power of Jesus Christ. That evidence is in a new life in Christ and verbal affirmation of what God has done in Jesus Christ in your life.

What is it that will attract your friends and relatives who are not Christians? A quiet confidence that arises out of your security as a person in Christ will attract them. A peace that is serene in the midst of turmoil and unrest will attract them. A love that is genuine and evidenced in loving concern with not even a trace of sentimentalism will attract them. All of these things are gifts of His grace given to you at the new birth. Now you need to work them out in Christian living. "So then, my beloved, just as you have always obeyed, not as in my presence only, but now much more in my absence, work out your salvation with fear and trembling; for it is God who is at work in you, both to will and to work for His good pleasure" (Philippians 2:12,13 NASB).

Be a good listener. A witness listens more than he talks. All of us resent the hard sell. When I go into a store, if a salesman begins to put pressure on me, I leave. I resent it when someone uses me or does not respect my personality and my right to make a free decision. If you listen to people they may tell you where they are hurting. Then you will be able to introduce them to Jesus Christ at the point of their need.

The greatest asset you have is Christlike love. Love never takes advantage of people by publicly embarrassing them. Love never tries to overpower people. Love has good manners. Love will, as Jesus did, speak to the person's need and not to his sin. Love will hear him out. When we love people, we see them not as people who need God, but people who are loved by God. No matter how sinful they are, God loves them. There is no need for you to tell them that God loves them if you do not genuinely and sincerely love them yourself. When people bare their hurt to you, it will be easy to apply the "balm of Gilead."

Begin with your relatives. More people are influenced for Christ by relatives than any other person or group. I have polled audience after audience in all parts of the country by asking them for a show of hands as to who was most influential in their becoming a Christian. Usually it turns out that about fifty-five per cent were influenced by an immediate relative, about twenty per cent by a Sunday school teacher, and about ten per cent by a pastor or other professional religious worker. The other fifteen per cent were influenced by other people. Only a very very small percentage came to Christ without the immediate assistance of another person.

Most people find it much easier to witness away from home. Remember that Jesus told the demoniac of Gadara to go home and witness. It may be easier away from home, but it is much more fruitful at home. Your relatives love you and that is a good beginning. They also know more about you than anyone else and that is an asset. Do not be intimidated by the fact that your relatives know your weaknesses. They also know what you were before the new birth and what you are now. The change God has made in your life may even anger them and cause them to rebuff your efforts to speak to them, but all the while they are watching and listening.

Pray regularly for your relatives who are not Christians. You can be used of God to bring them to Christ. At the witness of John the Baptist, Andrew stayed the night with Jesus Christ (perhaps under a friendly olive tree) and the next morning he found his brother, whom the whole world would come to know, and witnessed to him. "He found first his own brother Simon, and said, 'We have found the Messiah' (the Christ).' He brought him to Jesus" (John 1:41,42).

You must remember that you do not convert anyone. You do not "win" anyone. God does not hold you responsible for any person's salvation. That is their own responsibility. God holds you responsible for your witness. When you witness faithfully with your life and your lips, you must leave the results with God. You can ask people to open their lives to Jesus Christ, but you cannot open the door of their lives. That is something only they can do by an act of their will. The Holy Spirit is the only one who can convince persons that they are sinners and need a Savior. You cannot force a birth or do a spiritual cesarean section. People who are born spiritually are not born by the will of man. Leave all the results with God, including the credit for those who are born again. Never count converts as yours. They belong to God. You were only the instrument. "I planted, Apollos watered, but God caused the increase. So then neither the one who plants nor the one who waters is anything, but God who caused the increase. Now he who plants and he who waters are one; but each will receive his reward according to his own labor. For we are fellow workers with God" (I Corinthians 3:7-9). The reward is not according to the results, but according to the labor. You can work at witnessing.

What about the Church?

You may already be a part of the church. John Wesley was a member of and a minister of a church before he was born again. It may be that you need to stay in your church and witness to what God has done in your life. Many denominations and churches in those denominations once had very few people who claimed a new birth experience but now have a growing number. Your present church may afford one of the greatest opportunities possible for witness and ministry.

It is also possible that, like John Wesley, you find it impossible to work within the structure of your church and you may need to find another church where you are more comfortable. Never become the source of dissension in the church. If you feel that you have discovered something new and thrilling that others have not discovered, do not become filled with pride in what God has done and fall into a holier-than-thou attitude that will destroy your Christlikeness. Either work in the church with love and devotion or find one that is more suited to your new experience and your new life style in Christ. Remember that, if the church had been perfect, it ceased to be perfect the moment you became a member of it.

If you are not a member of the church, you need to do what the believers in the New Testament did when they were born again. "So then, those who had received his word [Peter's message on personal salvation] were baptized; and there were added that day about three thousand souls. And they were continually devoting themselves to the apostles' teaching and to fellowship, to the breaking of bread and to prayer . . . and they began selling their property and possessions, and were sharing them with all, as anyone might have need" (Acts 2:41,42,45 NASB). They committed themselves to the fellowship of the church. In baptism they were identified with Christ, with the church, and with the mission of Christ in the world. Jesus Christ had been baptized and they followed Him. They got involved in the teaching ministry of the fellowship. They sat together at the table of the Lord and broke bread and drank wine as He had taught them to do while He was with them. They identified themselves with the prayer life of the fellowship. They committed all of their possessions to Christ and shared life and life's possessions with the Christians who were in need.

Christ established the church and loves the church.

"Husbands, love your wives, just as Christ also loved the church and gave Himself up for her" (Ephesians 5:25 NASB). When you became a Christian by rebirth, you became a member of His body. Now you need to find a local fellowship of that body for body-life. The church has survived two thousand years of persecution, ridicule, hatred and even the poor testimony of some of its members. The church has made some dreadful mistakes, even to the point of torturing heretics and waging war, and by so doing denied Jesus Christ and crucified Him again. But the church has survived.

Remember that not everyone who is a member of the local organization or the denomination is a born again Christian. Many people are Christians by tradition or culture and not by experience. They are Christians only through the accident of the first birth and not by the miracle of new birth. Find the fellowship of a loving caring people and assist them in evangelizing every person who is not a born again Christian and in ministering to hurting, alienated people.

Remember, it was the church that produced David Livingston, "Ma" Slesslor, Albert Schweitzer, John Wesley, Dwight L. Moody, Billy Sunday and many, many more, known and unknown. The old conference minutes of the Methodist church gave information by using questions and answers. In the minutes for 1791 there is the following: "Question 10: Who have died this year? Answer: Wyatt Andrews, who died full of faith and the Holy Ghost. As long as he could ride, he travelled; and while he had breath, he praised God." That is not much to know about a man. But it is enough to make me wish I knew him. You can only meet people like that in the body-life of the church. You need the church and the church needs you. The church has outlived all of her critics. You cannot explain how, in the midst of persecution, discrimination and repression, the church continues and grows, without recognizing that this is His church and "the gates of hell shall not prevail against it."

The church is a fellowship of sinners saved by grace. If the church has weak members, they require all the more love and care. The church is not for the self-righteous. Jesus did not come into the world to call the righteous but sinners to repentance. Some people in the church are more mature as Christians than others. We have said previously that some members of the church organization may not be Christians at all. We should not attempt to separate the weeds from the wheat. He will do that when He comes.

Become a part of a local fellowship of believers. Love it. Serve in it. Minister in His name through it. Make your life an example for those who are weak. Support the church with your prayers. Share with fellow believers in a ministry of healing, preaching and teaching. Christ will someday "sanctify her, cleansing her by the washing of water with the Word, that He might give to Himself the church in all her glory, not having a single spot or wrinkle or flaw, but being holy and blameless" (Ephesians 5:26,27). You and I both want to be present on that day.

Be Patient with Yourself

Sometimes you grow impatient with your progress. You think that the maturing process is slow. Just when you think you are making progress, something happens and you think that you are still a babe in Christ. The change that Christ works in your life sometimes is so slow that you can hardly recognize it is happening. Remember that He took some raw, uncouth, rugged men and He admitted them to Himself and constant fellowship with Him. He poured His life

221

into them. The change began at once. Soon, they began doing and saying things that they could never have done had they not met and lived with Him. Deeper and deeper into their nature and personality He reached until slowly they began talking and acting like Him. Their manner became more gentle; their words became softer and more loving; and they acted in a less self-centered way. They touched lepers and loved sinners. They were angered by injustice and incensed by crippling poverty. Soon, when people saw them, they said, one to the other, "They have been with Jesus."

Be patient with yourself, love yourself and respect yourself. Never depreciate yourself or what He has done for you. Remember that Christ died for you and that makes you infinitely precious and worthwhile.

It takes time and patience to turn mulberry leaves into silk. It takes time and patience to cut the facets in a diamond. God is working on us. Hang out your little sign, "Be patient with me; God is not through with me yet."

Happy growing up, child of God.